T0161297

Towards
Wholeness

The Buddhist Society Trust is a distinguished
press in the United Kingdom which enriches lives around
the world by advancing the study and practice of Buddhism.
Its activities are supported by charitable contributions
from individuals and institutions.
For more information visit: info@thebuddhistsociety.org

Published by The Buddhist Society Trust
© 2018 by The Buddhist Society Trust
Text © The Zen Trust

The publisher gratefully acknowledges
the generous contribution to this book provided by
The Hokun Trust and The Zen Centre, London

ISBN: 978-0-901032-49-2 (The Buddhist Society Trust)

A catalogue record for this book is available from the British Library

Text by Myokyo Daiyu Zenji
Edited by Sarah Auld
Designed by Avni Patel

The line drawings based on Master Kuo-an's
original pictures are by Hugh Rance (see pages 36–60).

Printed in Padstow, Cornwall by TJ International

Towards
Wholeness

Translation and Commentary by the

Venerable Myokyo Daiyu Zenji

THE BUDDHIST SOCIETY TRUST

Fragrance
of the Dharma
Hōkun Trust

THE
ZEN
CENTRE

CONTENTS

Foreword

THE BOOK IS SHORT, a mere two hundred and forty pages of text, yet the subject matter enfolds those things most deep and profound in us. That are beyond us, and yet, at the same time are the most intimate. In the words of the author 'inborn in us is a longing or yearning that cannot be denied. Where it is directed to, or what it is directed at, we cannot know.' Here we are given a map, a guidebook, that uses a variety of sources to bring us back to 'the place where our own feet stand', from where the journey begins and where it ends. The author devoted the greater part of her life to the study and teaching of Zen Buddhism both in Japan and in England where she established two training monasteries. However the book is not only confined to the orthodoxies of Buddhism but covers in a vast sweep, both ancient mythology, the great world religions from East and West as well as insights derived from the great figures of the twentieth century such as C G Jung. This does not mean that Buddhism is neglected, far from it, but it is that looking at Buddhism, and in particular through the lens of our universal and shared mythological and religious history that the mystery and insights of Buddhism are brought vividly to life. And it is not just Buddhism, although this is the warp and weft of the text, but also Zen training and in particular the Rinzai line of Zen.

However the book can be read by anyone of any faith, religion or culture, with an interest and genuine longing to know what lies beneath the shallow veneer of consciousness. Once caught sight of, the book will hopefully act as a catalyst to explore further and deeper. This aspect of the book points to the universal understanding that we all have, but are unaware of, and goes far beyond the narrow confines of race, religion and nation, and points towards that which truly unites us as human beings, the shared human heart, that feels pain and loss, joy and sorrow, and yet transcends at the same time its own individual boundary, and in that transcendence unites us all.

The book catches the style and flavour of Venerable Myokyo-ni's teaching as well as her interests and concerns, pointing as always to that place 'where our own feet stand'.

Desmond Biddulph
President, The Buddhist Society
London, 2018

Chapter One

The Quest for Wholeness

THIS EARTH WE LIVE ON, and of which we are part, is itself part of the solar system. And this is but a speck in the outer reaches of the Milky Way. Stippled on the night sky that frames as a window our vision outwards, the Milky Way traverses heaven. Its beginning and end are outside our vision; the extent of the universe we cannot conceive. Yet we are part of it; the same laws shaped us, are inherent in us, and we are subject to them. The urge to find out is also the longing to find ourselves, to become aware of the relatedness.

The circumambulation of the earth around the sun marks for us a time unit, our year, with its swing of the seasons, and gives us the sense of time, awareness of coming to be and ceasing to be, and renewal which is also evolution, development. The spin of the earth on its way round the sun gives the experience of light and dark, of waking and sleep, of work and rest, of awareness in the light, of dreaming in sleep. We see by the light, as far as our eyes can reach. But in the darkness, the star- spangled sky murmurs of things beyond our ken, outside our conscious perceptions and bounds, stirs in us that which we are without knowing, and to which we naturally incline.

In our little daily round of bestirring ourselves and getting tired, we lose sight of this relatedness in which we have our being and without which the sap of life dries up in us. So from of old we have had recourse to symbols that remind us of our relatedness and the ground of being, evoke it in us ever again. We know these symbols as the attributes of the Divine; by them it is intuited. And whatever name or names we may give to the Divine, the Divine itself, its essence or nature we do not and cannot know for it is nothing separate from or outside us.

We are not divorced from it, though we cannot see it. Just as we cannot know Life itself, except by living it.

Words like Life, or the Divine, are names, abstractions to conceptualize an inkling, an inherent sense which has the power to move us. And the part of us or in us that is so moved is also variously designated. But if we are aware of being moved and responding, we will not need to take our stand on words but recognize it under all its names. The word 'spirit' for that which moves, and 'soul' for what is moved by it, are familiar from of old, but we need to be careful for they have for us Christian connotations which do not necessarily apply.

'The soul is naturally religious.' But when the living spirit is lost, a dead shell remains and words become empty of meaning; the spirit, moving as it listeth, has gone elsewhere. The living spirit must move. If its proper channels are blocked, its springs are sanded over, then under the wasteland the spirit labours. It begins to rise like a flood, forces itself into runnels and fills forms unsuitable to its nature. Then a political creed or trendy 'ism', however naive, commonplace, or lurid the formulation, suddenly seems to be imbued with all the attributes of the Divine, with the overwhelming fascination of the spirit.

Or more neutrally, when appropriate forms are missing, then like a shimmering veil the intensity of the spirit drapes itself over the inferior and unfitting object and so deceives us. How can the spirit deceive? Or do we deceive ourselves because we cannot differentiate the numinosity of the risen spirit from the banal object onto which it has projected itself perforce, lacking appropriate channels, symbols? So we get dazzled and blinded. Then like a will-o'-the-wisp on a swamp or a mirage in the desert, the spirit does not quicken but leads to strife and destruction.

These alluring by-passes beckon and entice especially in times when traditional values are lost and there is unrest and disorientation, and lack of humility. Just such times as we live in now.

There is nothing new about a will-o'-the-wisp, or a mirage; they are well-authenticated phenomena, their causes are understood. But we still succumb to them, and to the equally well-known and authenticated inner or spiritual by-passes; however much they shift their shapes to emerge again under new names, there is nothing new about them.

As water seeks gradients to flow along, the soul seeks the spirit. 'Soul' is an awkward term these days. It is not a known entity, it has no form; its existence can be rationally denied. The familiar Christian connotation is different from what the Romans meant by 'anima', the animate or essential part, that which enlivens. It reaches beyond the narrow confines of the separate individual, it is the breath of life, and opens up into relatedness to what is. This would also mean emerging out of the alienation of a lonely, separate 'I', and the finding of true identity which is only possible by adequate relation to the living spirit.

If the meaning of religion is considered in its original, pre-Christian connotation of religio, then its function is seen as a re-linking of an individual separate 'I' with one's ground of being, with the matrix from which one comes and to which one returns, not in a blotting out but as a fulfilment, as water rises up from the sea but irresistibly seeks its way back home again. An alienated 'I' fears this homecoming, and actually is that fear. The re-linking that is effected on a religious way removes this fear, the 'I'-alienation, and thus restores the birthright to the individual. With that truly understood, most problems are solved. This is the promise that such a re-linking holds out.

The question is how to forge such a re-linking today, in the absence of spiritual and cultural values, and without falling victim to the ever-prevalent phenomenon of alluring by-passes, false spirituality. How to choose? The right sort always bears the hallmark of good quality. Good quality sells itself to the discerning eye; what is glitteringly wrapped up – well, that is good salesmanship; it need not be good quality. Also, whether we like it or not, good quality is connected with time and effort spent. And something ineffable but strangely homelike clings to it, an unspectacular simplicity which fits, which is not contrived or strained but natural.

Attempts to catch, to possess the living spirit are always connected with shoddy, inadequate containers and are bound to fail. The spirit is the possession of no one; moreover, the attributes of the Divine, such as tremendous, awe-inspiring, overwhelming, point unmistakably to its enormous energy potential which can blind, burn and shatter as well as brighten, warm and strengthen. It depends on the receiving end – us. A law seems to operate to the effect that the more unfitting the receiving vessel – not only my crude appetites but even more so my notions, views and ideals – the greater the deception by the spirit, which then acts destructively.

So, on closer inspection the function of religion may be seen as preparing us so that a re-linking may take place without major mishap. The more alienated I, the receiving end, the more preparation, that is, time and effort is required.

In an age like ours, where genuine religious values have lost their meaning, it is perhaps difficult to see that this preparation has a twofold function, or deals with the two possible requirements of an individual. Firstly, it binds, knits the single individual into his place as a responsible member of his community and its professed spiritual values; related and re-linked, the individual life and one's individual lot have thus meaning and purpose within a larger context, both in the secular and in the religious sphere, and so the heart knows contentment even amid strife and struggle, for it is not alienated from its home base. I am no longer out in the cold, a kind of displaced person in an alien, and to me, meaningless environment that bears no relation to me nor I to it. Something like this seems to be the step we all must take, work and prepare for – not only for our own sake and wellbeing but for the sake of all of us.

But as there have always been, there always will be those who cannot settle for just that. There is something in some individuals that urges them to further unfoldment, not against but over the commonality and its bonds. This second step, seen from the side of the community as a freeing from its bonds, is not a revolt against it for which it is cheaply mistaken when effort towards knitting in has never been made. This effort, however, seems to be the pre-condition, the good quality factor, that renders the individual capable of exposing his nakedness to the proximity of the spirit. The one safety factor in this highly dangerous undertaking is utter nakedness, an 'I' shorn of all attributes and accretions, the innocence of a little child. 'Unless you become as little children' – which is very different from being merely childish! I do not naturally come by this nakedness, and so the freeing function of religion is a way of helping the individual to let go again of those attributes that he had to work so hard to acquire. Not the attributes, but the strength that was fashioned in their acquisition, is now needed as staying power when the attributes are peeled off. All traditions show this stripping process as a hard way indeed. When nothing remains of I except strength of endurance, the living spirit can be approached and a merging take place which re-structures and widens the personality. In Buddhist parlance, this is the way that starts from the delusory 'I', leads through No-I which is experienced as death, the Great Death to Life, and then to conscious awareness of the living web of totality, the Buddha-nature, the True Face before father and mother were born, when the individual wave becomes aware of its ocean nature, of its being ocean. In Christian symbolism Christ is seen as being both the son of God and the son of Man. The Jungian concept of individuation shows it as the shift from 'I' to Self.

Since the difficulties are obvious, need it be stressed that it is rarely realized in its fullness? Figures like Buddha or Jesus stand out like beacons over millennia. We need to acknowledge distances. If all is the same, why bestir ourselves? If we want everything at our own level, we must tear down all that is more. A mass society robs the individual of his dignity; but connected with dignity, like head and tail of a coin, is humility. Their opposites, lack of identity and overweening pretensions hold sway today. Do we even suspect that our irreligious mass society, in flagrant contradiction of the Christian message and ethic, is regressing not only to classical antiquity where at least the free householder had a soul, the dignity of an individual, but to sheer barbarity with a despot whose subjects are expendable chattels? Do we wonder that Christianity, that gave a soul, the dignity and uniqueness of an individual, to every man, woman and slave, spread like wildfire in times that knew no mass media, no telly, no radio, no newspapers, and when the fastest speed news could travel by was that of a galloping horse? Have we ever understood the religion that has shaped our culture and that our forebears at least professed for generations? Have we had no inkling that the message was to love our neighbour as ourselves – and that this has less to do with the neighbour and more to do with ourselves? Have we learned to truly love ourselves in the sense of at least accepting and tolerating ourselves rather than heedlessly serving the idol of what I think I am and want?

These are pertinent questions, for charity starts at home. A Chinese proverb says that even a journey of a thousand miles starts right under one's feet. How can I safely set out on a journey which entails direction if I do not know where my feet stand? We would like to run without the bother of learning to walk, and we are prone to the fine gesture, throwing out the baby with the bathwater. But the way to the spirit, which is the way of the spirit, is not the grand gesture, but a patient and painstaking way, step by step; a way of divestiture, not a way of accretion.

Though this way has many names, it is but One Way. Experienced and described differently by different wayfarers, with different landmarks and stages set out by different traditions, it is the same way, and walking upon it taxes all pilgrims with the same difficulties, and opens the same vistas to all travellers.

Chapter Two

Reflections

THERE IS A ZEN SAYING, 'In the trackless, the path comes to an end'. To the trackless, there are many paths. However divergent these may seem to be, the actual walkers find much common ground and familiar stages along these well-worn paths. This side of the great divide, the territory is well explored and can be described. No genuine lore of the Way will describe the 'other shore'; it will only point towards it in simple analogies and leave it at that. For good measure, it will also warn not to mistake the finger pointing to the moon for the moon itself. But the very existence of this lore is an attempt to share with others so interested gleanings of an essence, of a spirit or principle that permeates everything.

Inborn in us is a longing or yearning that cannot be denied. Where it is directed to, or what it is directed at, we cannot know. But it forces us to form some picture or idea, and towards that it forces us to strive. This pictured 'goal' may vary from heavenly kingdom to new car, but is actually a misconceived image of this longing as it reflects itself in me. The energy content of the yearning seems then lodged in the image which now fatally attracts me. 'If only I can attain that, I'll be happy – that is, fulfilled – ever after!' This image drapes itself like a shimmering veil over a carrier – car, person, idea. It may be short-lived or long lasting, but fulfilment cannot be found in its possession. Once attained, the veil thins and the attraction soon pales. What the heart truly longs for, I cannot see because of the image-veil. Like the hues of a rainbow, the images break the one light and make us strive after one colour out of the whole. This chasing after rainbow colours is considered a fundamental mistake in Buddhism. Selection of one colour and striving after it is separation, apart from rather than part of what is. The one who sets this chain of mistakes into action is I, my selecting, my choosing. It leads ever further away into alienation. What the heart longs for is its own wholeness, reflection without selection, clear seeing of what is, the manifold that is one but not the same.

Thus, if I mistake myself as separate and alone, I must go chasing after the rainbow. The dilemma is that I myself cannot know wholeness, yet the inborn striving is directed toward wholeness and fulfils itself in it. The correction, which is also the end of my alienation, is the end of 'I' as I know myself.

Our culture, directed outwards, seems to suffer increasingly from this one-sided direction, and whatever is dimly conceived as the corrective movement, is merely a swing to the opposite extreme and just as one-sided. Wholeness, however, is all embracing. It is also a tremendous force that beckons – just this yearning or longing that will give us no peace. Strive we must. If we can desist from making graven images of it, from seeking it in pictures outside, we become aware of its working in us. In the Diamond Sutra, the Buddha warns, 'If you seek me in form, search for me in sound, you have gone astray and cannot see the Tathagata.'

Desisting from the making of pictures, however, makes us suffer, suffer from the lack of fulfilment, from a general dissatisfaction; we become aware of the restlessness inside us and of our times, or are woken up in the small hours by a tiny voice that whispers that something is missing and urges toward unfoldment, towards inner growth.

We are Westerners, and our age is irreligious. We no longer understand religious language, not even our own – less so when expressed by symbols and idioms foreign to our mentality. A careful and sensitive approach is indicated. For this, the Analytical Psychology of C G Jung can be extremely helpful (see Chapter 5). It is a conducive, reflecting mirror, of our own mentality and basic assumptions, deals with our own humdrum problems and difficulties, and points a way out. In that, it provides a means of decoding foreign language into what is familiar and constant in human experience, hence also in ours, thus translating from the dazzling, exotic and weird to the workable home ground.

The traditional form of Zen training is perhaps an ideal complement to our top-heavy, head-only approach. It insists on incorporating the body, training with the body, in everyday life. Its concrete training analogies bring home little by little an awareness of the aridity of mental gymnastics and intellectual juggling. With this comes an insight that the stripping away of 'I'-accretions – as when I cannot have my way and must give in – liberates energy. This happens when conflicts are contained and endured in full awareness, without refusal or shying away, and without losing the human quality of gentleness. In its extreme form, this is the Passion of Christ. Little passions are our workaday training ground. These, suffered through, again and again, result in a genuine change of both I and the energy that has risen and for which we employ the same word, in the plural, the passions. It is the transformation of the wild, passionate energy which constitutes the work, the training: transformation from its primitive aspect as we encounter it in our wilder outbursts, through its subtler forms as opinionated obstinacy, to its humanization, and from there to the religious pole of its spiritualization.

As a religion, Buddhism functions both to bind the individual into his cultural/social context, and to free him seemingly from just that, but factually from all his own attributes and accretions. The former aspect we are unfamiliar with; it is not in our own background; and it is difficult for us nowadays to understand how our Christianity, in the days when we still had faith in it, influenced and informed our daily life. Only in ordinary language do we still find a trace, when we exclaim only too often, 'Oh, God!', as if we still took refuge in Him, or when love or fear of God prevented us from acting against His principles. This freeing aspect of Buddhism is what inclines us to it in the first place, and though that is particularly stressed in Zen Buddhism, without being well grounded in the former, the disciplinary aspect of the religious life, our attempts toward the freeing aspect will be in vain.

The Way is concerned with the individual, with 'I', for that is how the individual experiences himself, to start with. Its approach goes through well-mapped territory. The maps show, however, that there are equally well worn and alluring tracks that just peter out, lead nowhere, and leave the traveller stranded or worse.

In Buddhism, I am a delusion, and this delusion grasps at, is fatally attracted to – or repelled by – anything that beckons, promises or shimmers. Deluded, the beckoning of the imperative towards wholeness is then seen in the glittering of fools' gold, the exotic, the odd, the slick, facile and quick. Jungian psychology provides a Westerner with some homely, matter-of-fact truths that counteract flights of fancy. We do well to consider it carefully if we feel attracted to an Eastern way such as Zen Buddhism. Both stress that energy, endurance, courage and staying power are required for development. Both have ways to take in raw material and to help towards shaping itself as a first step, and then towards growth as its own nature demands. In Jungian terminology these two steps are called 'adaptation' and 'individuation'. From which, incidentally, we may learn that the Zen Way proper, like Jungian individuation, is not a cure for the neurotic, for whom the required energy is blocked and who needs to be cured, adapted and collected, before he can embark on a further development, should his nature require it.

In a broader sense, adaptation is the unfoldment of the past in the present, of what is. We cannot live in yesterday. And development is growing forward into the future which is as yet not formed – an unknown adventure. These seemingly two vectors reflect two movements inherent in our dual world, thus also in us. One could not be without the other. As such, they do not exist, but in us are differentiated as principles of orientation, both outside and inside. One is the horizontal with its cyclic changes of 'coming to be, ceasing to be' and the renewal, as every spring brings back its blossoms, and which we can call and have called 'Mother Nature'. The other component we somehow conceive of as a vertical; along it renewal means not the same but change, not reformation but trans-formation, development, evolution. This vertical component, urge or pull, we might call 'Father Spirit'. These two, Earth and Heaven, are our basic, primal perceptions of a Divine Pair. Or, turning round, the Divine becomes perceptible to us as this primal pair.

What the Divine itself is we can neither define nor express, nor know, though our picture-making propensity has rendered it in divers shapes and conceived all kinds of dwelling places for it. What we can say of it, however, is that it has the power to touch and move us, to spring us out of our inertia and selfishness, and to make us strive for a reunion with it. This reunion also has two aspects, with 'ceasing to be' common to both. One is death, when the manifested form returns home, just as the individual wave loses itself in what it always has been – ocean. The other is transformation, equally a return home, when the individual wave becomes aware of its ocean nature, aptly called spiritual rebirth, preceded by the death of I, The Great Death. To awaken from the delusion of 'I'-hood as from a dream re-links us with what we have always been. We are pointed towards this reunion, however often we mistake the pointing finger for the moon, the urge for a graven image of our own fashioning, an idea for the real.

The reunion is a conscious becoming aware of the harmonious cooperation with our ground of being, with those two vectors operating in us as well as around us and in which we are embedded and at home, their children as well as husbandmen, their agents and shapers. If that is achieved in conscious awareness, the veil is rent and being itself has become conscious in us, can use our eyes and behold itself. The realization that 'I and my Father are one' is at-one-ment.

This divine pair has many names; the most neutral ones are inertia and energy, matter and spirit. Differentiated, they are seen as a pair of opposites, which can be further detailed as three, four or many. As two they are complementary; in fact they are indivisibly one. The Zen question is relevant: 'When all returns to one, where does the one return to?'

The Eastern conception of manifestation and re-absorption of form has never lost sight of inherent divinity. However, human nature being one-sided, there the repetitive, cyclic process is stressed. This gives rise to the difficulty that though individual release from the recurring process is possible, the scheme of things remains ever unchanged, is timeless; it reforms endlessly but is not itself subject to transformation.

This is summarized in the Buddhist formulation of the Wheel of Being, which is a kind of chart of the aspects of existence. It shows us to be in the grip of impermanence or change – characteristically portrayed as a demon rather than spirit and it is set in motion by the Three Fires of desire, anger and delusion. Yet this conception contains an insight that eludes a cursory glance. It portrays faithfully the status quo, the basic delusion of a separate entity, of 'I', from which we suffer.

Since I cling to the known and am frightened of the 'totally unknown', real change in the sense of total transformation terrifies me and so this change is, from the side of I, correctly pictured as a demon. Release from this Wheel is possible only from the human state. Since this is the only one with a sense of I, it hints at something unknown to I but towards which all existence strives.

The Three Fires of desire, anger and delusion which set the Wheel in motion are crude, primal energy, and its valid transformation is what all practice is concerned with. Thus release from the cyclic Wheel is a true change of attitude. With this the Wheel itself assumes another dimension which is not conceivable to I. Nothing is stated about it; it is only hinted at by showing the crucial factors, I and fear. The consequence of genuine transformation is human warmth that radiates and shines of itself, as the sun does, needing no object to shine upon, for shining is its nature.

In Jungian parlance, the term for this aspect of energy is 'psychic energy', as distinct from physical energy. We watch these two forces at play within us, for example on a dark, cold winter morning, in our reaction to the alarm clock and the struggle between 'I ought to get up' and 'just one more minute'. The physical energy to get up is there but the psychic energy that activates it into motion is in abeyance until 'fired' by need. However, the tremendous, balled force of this energy, when it touches us, we have always experienced as awesome, and other, and given it the attribute of the Divine, Godhead. Whatever our conception of it may be, it has the power to move us deeply. It has always exacted from us at least reverence and obedience, and in closer proximity to it, awe. This response is not out of date, rather a healthy reaction to that which can so deeply move us that it forces a total transformation, and a *mysterium tremendum* (Rudolf Otto, *The Holy*, trans. J W Harvey, 1936) can strike us with holy terror. Religious formulations, though invariably symbolic, are yet very accurate. As we may read in the Bible, whenever an angel or divine messenger appears and addresses a mortal, he invariably starts with the words, 'Fear not'.

The ghostly otherness and tremendous force of the spirit shatters a stiff-necked 'I'. Hence the insistence on bowing in all religious traditions, the age-old gesture of hands folded in supplication and devotion – not for what I can get, for that, too, is a sin against the Holy Ghost – but to soften myself, to render myself innocuous, and make the soul receptive to its own home. Without this true humility, any attempt to approach the living spirit is bound to end in misfortune – a warning that all traditions contain. 'Who is near unto Me is near unto the fire'.

I may not lift the veil, can only bow and revere. Then the spirit may prompt, may beckon, to undertake the long journey of transformation, to go into what is most fearsome, and through it find the way home. Naked again as one was born, the veil of the delusion of being a separate entity, alienated from what is, drops. But as different from when one was born, there is now the conscious awareness of reunion, and living in and by it.

Chapter Three

Zen Buddhism

ZEN BUDDHISM is a religious way and as such, in common with other religious ways of training, it has the usual basic framework of discipline, religious observances, contemplation and work.

As a Buddhist School, it is based on the fundamentals of the Buddha's teaching. The Three Signs of Being are Impermanence, Suffering and No-I. It is I who suffer, suffer from the delusion of being a separate entity, wanting my way, resisting change when it does not suit me, etc. This alienates me from what is and what I am a part of, robs me of relationship with it. Hence I suffer from lack of identity, loneliness, am unfulfilled, not whole, and long for a way out. The longing is genuine, but what I long for in my separateness is delusive. A part cannot become the whole; too much would remain outside. I cannot incorporate the world.

The urge towards growth is inherent in all that is. It is the tragedy and perhaps the grandeur of the human state that I, in my I-delusion, disobey it and try to use its tremendous energy for my purpose or benefit, rather than for a re-linking of myself to Being, which is wholeness: hence the Buddhist teaching, its stress on No-I, to shift the attention into this wholesome direction.

As long as I persist in my delusion of being 'I', that tremendous energy which prompts towards growth and unfoldment turns wild. The more I insist on my way, the more primitive, the more elemental it becomes. In Buddhism this energy, fierce and hot as we know it in our passionate emotions, is aptly likened to a roaring fire. Three main channels of this are distinguished, and it is referred to as the Three Fires, of desire, of anger and of delusion. The delusion is I, resistor rather than conductor. So the Fires flare.

We do not merely suffer from the objective outside, from what is unavoidable like a toothache, or from situations or persons. What we really suffer from are our own emotional reactions against them.

The Buddha himself summed up his teaching as, 'Suffering I teach and the Way out of it.' Suffer we all do. Suffering is our faithful companion, physically and mentally. Physically such as a toothache, illness, pain, and death that awaits us all; mentally we feel unease and unrest, sorrow, grief at parting, frustration at unfulfilled wants and needs, and fear of becoming no-thing when we so much want to be some-thing. The delusion and source of suffering is in that.

The cure or alleviation of suffering is nowadays the province of medicine. Yet even in our irreligious time, a chaplain regularly visits a hospital. The mental component, today considered psychological, is properly the sphere of religion, the 'cure of souls'. There is close interaction between physical and mental suffering; the sufferer's own attitude to his pain is an important contributing factor for both the occurrence of the illness and its cure.

The artificial split into mind and body has greatly misled us, the more so as I usually align myself with my mind in opposition to the body which I either despise, or out of which I endeavour to get infinite gratification for my (hence insatiable) wants, much to the detriment of both the body and me. The old Christian classification of body, soul, and spirit is a useful one; from a Buddhist point of view, none of them is I or mine, but together they compromise wholeness.

Joy and sorrow are constants in human experience. Both are fleeting, as are all particular, manifested forms. Nothing lasts, all changes. We have no difficulty in accepting a joy that comes our way; rather we cling to it as if it were our property, and suffer its loss. So our attitude to suffering is the first crucial step in the process of becoming whole.

Since Buddhism teaches the Middle Way, it goes without saying that extremes need alleviation; they do not constitute a training ground. But great things have small beginnings. Hence, to start with, our attitude to suffering embraces first the small things in our daily life, those that niggle, irk, irritate, frustrate, the little hurts and wounds.

We usually try to avoid them, to turn away from them, refuse them; and if these techniques are to no avail, we become bitter about them, and stress symptoms set in. The new attitude to be cultivated is to accept that one suffers, and rather than looking for distraction from it, willingly live it while getting on with one's daily chores. Thus this particular little suffering can be lived through, which is both its cure and a contribution to the process of becoming whole. Refusing it, we refuse part of life; unlived life then piles up against us, as fear and threat. We have only the repressed symptoms which will emerge again; the cause is not even touched. That, too, is part of the delusion; to believe that one gets rid of suffering by refusing it.

And so it seems that in suffering, our own attitude of not refusing, but of accepting and living it, is crucial. 'Take up your cross and walk.' Buddhism recognizes the fact of suffering and suggests ways of alleviating it, facing it, bearing it, in short, accepting it and making wholesome use of it. This is a positive attitude and because of that, Buddhism is not overly concerned with the ever-changing symptoms but treats the cause itself, asserting that it can be eradicated: hence the Buddha's 'Way out of Suffering' by living suffering when it arises.

Our world consists of light and dark; we are part of it. If we select and cling to the light only, we cannot grow whole; we are then merely threatened by the dark. If we live the suffering that life presents us with and which is constant in human experience, not only will suffering decrease because it is not embellished by our resistance; it will also affect the sufferer himself, who becomes all-embracing. Just this is the road toward wholeness on which the religious sense emerges of itself because on it the individual is weaned from excessive 'I'-ness.

Thus, in conformity with the Buddhist principles, training in Zen Buddhism is concerned with 'I', as I am driven by the Fires. But since I am fortunately not always ablaze, training in daily life means the cultivation of a new attitude, of giving myself as wholly and totally as I can to what I am doing at the moment. Just that. And whenever I become aware that I have been deflected again, without any further ado, resolutely coming back to, giving myself to what I am doing. Not 'I do' but 'I give myself into the doing.' Truly cultivated, the consequences of this are so far-reaching that it could be said that only this is needed, if we could but perfect it. Lack of attention and the Fires deflect me again and again. Hence the need for training.

A Mahayana (Northern Branch of Buddhism) saying states that the passions are the Buddha-nature, and vice versa. Not, of course, in their respective manifestations, but basically they are that same tremendous energy. Like all energy, it functions by sliding along gradients from pole to pole, or on finding an outlet, it discharges itself in action. Though blind impulse also releases this energy, its action is out of phase with the situation, is elemental and compulsive. If I tread on a poisonous snake, it bites when I inadvertently come too near it. This is the old compulsion or instinctive reaction, when on a sudden encounter he who hits first is the more likely to survive. But this unconscious primitive state no longer holds for us human beings – if running round a corner, I suddenly bump into you, I don't just hit out. Yet when one is startled, the impulse to do so is there; and the human quality is to be conscious of it and yet not to be carried away by it.

It may be said that what is at stake in Zen training is a valid transformation of this emotional energy from its blind, wild compulsion at the primitive end of the pole, up the scale of humanization to the spiritual end of the pole, the Buddha-nature or the Buddha-heart.

In Buddhism, thought, speech and action are considered as one; thought gives rise to speech and action. Unconscious resentment may carry a greater charge than slamming a door. As an aspect of the whole force of life, emotional energy is of tremendous power. The more unaware I am, or the more I cling to my rational side only, the more blindly the energy works in and through me. Hence awareness of and containing it is a concern of Zen training.

All traditions have their symbolic renderings of this situation. There seems to be an urge towards evolution and wholeness, from organic sludge to us, or more poetically rendered, for Being to see itself, that is to become aware of itself. Thus the 'I' is a mediator that cannot be dispensed with, though it is also the object of transformation. In the course of Zen training, both the emotional energy and I change as they interact.

The Buddha, a man who by his own efforts awoke from the basic delusion as from a dream, realized that he had 'rediscovered an ancient path leading to an ancient city' – the way that leads to the heart, one's own. Only the heart has warmth; this is the other facet or aim of Zen training, together with the clear seeing.

The emotions have always been connected with the heart. The persistent mistranslation of this crucial Buddhist concept of 'heart' as 'mind' has obscured the process, made it unintelligible, and given rise to the mental gymnastics of I trying to pull myself up by my bootlaces, as ever stirred into action by the Three Fires. This mistranslation of 'mind' has also veiled the difficulties of the process, and obstructs warmth and beauty, the 'common to us all' factor, and thus its humanity.

Mind is the instrument of reason, hard-won in our evolution. One of our most useful assets is a clear, cool mind. This works of itself unless interfered with, 'fired', that is, blocked or blinded by emotions. During active Zen training, we are therefore little concerned with the mind, but mostly with the heart, particularly with its wild, emotional aspect.

For sheer survival, man has from the earliest times developed means to deal with emotional outbreaks. Whether hunting a mammoth or driving a car, a person so engaged cannot afford an emotional outburst that carries him away, incapacitates him however briefly. Forceful disciplines to control the emotions have turned out to be inadequate in the long run. Emotions are capable of forcing their way through all 'blind' attempts at control (repression), either in primitive eruptions, or in psychosomatic symptoms; while repressed, life seems empty and meaningless. Moreover, if and when the emotions are repressed or rejected, work with them and on them, their transformation, is not possible. And when discharged in an emotional explosion, the precious energy is wasted.

This places a tremendous responsibility on the individual who, willing to see, is forced to accept his own emotionality as it portrays itself in his reactions, and to consciously, and willingly endure the conflict while continuing to function smoothly in his everyday activities. This double action or inter-action is the transforming agent.

Hence the training discipline needs to be voluntarily undertaken and carried out in order to be effective. It is not exacted in order to control or cut off emotions, but consti-tutes a framework against which the individual reacts, thus becoming familiar with his emotional household. The reli-gious attitude of acceptance helps one to endure emotional stress, from which accrues the strength to continue function-ing in awareness. Thus the individual I and the emotions, both undergo a slow but sure change. A religious attitude also prevents the ever-present danger of I appropriating the newly found strength for selfish purposes. As in all good husbandry this energy needs to be ploughed back into the practice so that it may deepen and ripen, and bear much fruit.

What the Zen school radically insists on is the courage of basic honesty, resulting in genuine insight. And what it radically refutes is intellectual juggling, bandying of fancy words, and empty imitation. Its seeming iconoclasm does not repudiate the Buddhist teachings, but the mere lip service to them without the relevant insight. In Zen language, this is called mistaking the finger pointing at the moon for the moon.

For good measure it adds the homely warning that a fish the size of a house does not flit about in a mountain brook!

In conformity with all Buddhism, the Zen School holds that the hard shell of I want it, as it suits me, as it ought to be, as I won't have it, think right, etc., is a mistaken combination, hardened or 'baked' by the Three Fires into a false identity. The hard shell needs to be ground off, which is slow and patient work; brute shattering from outside or inside spells catastrophe. When ready, the new attitude, re-linked, emerges of itself and can unfold. Since sloughing off the last vestiges of the old shell, and the new emergence, is a difficult process, not without danger, a guide is needed to ensure genuine transformation. The homely analogy for this is a hen hatching out her eggs. When the chick is ready to come out, when the time is ripe, the hen pecks the shell to help the chick to emerge.

Since the shell of 'I', my brittleness, is connected with the emotions, a real re-structuring in depth is possible only when both I and the emotions are engaged, and the resulting conflict is suffered patiently and in full awareness.

This process or labour has been portrayed in the analogy of the Bull-herding Pictures. In them is shown, carefully and accurately, the searching for, finding, catching and gentling of the heart-bull, and the further transformation of the energy he stands for: wild and wilful, the primitive aspect of our heart, the surging emotions which make our problems, whether they beset us as sheer passion or more subtly, invade our views, opinions, and convictions, and further pervert them. It is due to the emotional content that, when our opinions are disputed, we lose our coolness and see red, the colour the bull goes for! A bull is not exactly a herdable animal – which hints at the labour and effort necessary for the enterprise. The would-be herdsman is I, as I think I am and know myself when I set out on the quest. We do not know what we truly want, yet search we must – but we do not expect a bull! But there is an inalienable connection between the two, which the pictures show clearly. Both bull and herdsman change in the process of training.

The Bull-herding Pictures, being typically Eastern, posit nothing. They merely point at a transformation process that takes place in the heart when the analogous requirements are met and fulfilled.

Chapter Four

The Bull-Herding Series

STAGES ALONG A WAY are not the way itself. Pictures of those stages, however elaborate the captions, can at best point towards, but fail to give the flavour of, the actual journey, the experience, travail and labour of such wayfaring. Along it, the man changes as well as the Bull. With this firmly in mind, such pictures may be taken as signposts for travellers, to help their orientation. They are misleading if taken as an armchair travelogue.

The preface to the text begins: 'The real source of all the Buddhas is the original nature of all that lives.' It is our essence. Our inborn yearning, if we do not mistake it for what I want, urges us towards a re-linking with this essence. So we set out on our quest.

Picture 1 – The Search for the Bull

The part strives towards the whole; it becomes whole when subsumed in the whole. In that merger the part is not obliterated, which is the great fear I have. The part awakens as from a dream, has become aware of wholeness, is once more re-linked.

So the would-be herdsman, I, sets out on the search for the Heart-bull, looking for him everywhere, but failing to find him. Of that magnificent Bull it is said that he fills heaven and earth; how can it be so difficult to find him? Where could he hide himself? The herdsman started confidently, and yet the days pass without a trace of the Bull, and every evening, tired, the man faces the disappointment of the day's search.

It is not easy to see that which one believes to be a great thing or a great value, in something commonplace, despised or feared. What is important for this quest is continuity of effort and the facing of failure again and again. A real tempering takes place in the man, both on account of the effort made, and because its fruitlessness deflates the searcher. At this stage, only one thing matters, to continue without flagging.

What counts here is the effort spent.

Picture 2 – Seeing the Traces

'Many look for the Bull, but few ever have seen him'. Yes, this great endeavour takes great, almost fierce courage, and demands great endurance. The herdsman set out with a picture of the Bull in his mind. He watches himself – which only drives the Bull away. Look at the lines in the palm of your hand; to see them, there must be distance. When the hand closes over the eyes nothing is seen, but the impact is felt, experienced. Yet we must look for the Bull, clearly see his traces. The herdsman, caught between what he should and should not do, between what is right and wrong, 'turns round and round in the small cave' of his mental prison. The Bull meanwhile disports himself elsewhere, or, wily as he is, surreptitiously invades the man's mental processes and fires his notions and convictions.

To sit down in this cave would be stagnation; opinions, fancies of mind, all pictures, must be left and the search continued. Out of frustration, despair and exhaustion, anger suddenly flares up and infuses energy. This is the moment – does the herdsman see?

A way can only be learned by walking it. In time comes awareness of and familiarity with one's reactions, and so all of a sudden the man stumbles upon some traces and recognizes them as the Bull's. Off the man goes with fresh vigour, following the traces of that tremendous, wild thing. But though he finds a maze of traces now, the Bull is hiding from sight. He runs, trying to get a glimpse, trying to see, blunders around in the wilderness where the Bull roams – behind this bush, round that rock, surely now up yonder mountain? As he hurriedly scrambles up, the Bull has already run down the other side into a lush valley. The herdsman rushes after.

Picture 3 – Seeing the Bull

TOWARDS WHOLENESS

In the hot pursuit, the man gets himself worked up. His efforts and the Bull's combine, there is a glimpse, but the Bull is already gone. From now on, however, the man knows what he is after; he is no longer side-tracked into the by-passes of where and the wildernesses of what. And now he is really after the Bull. He knows him, not just his bellowing. The Bull can no longer hide himself fully. But though the herdsman has glimpsed the Bull, they are yet widely apart. However, having once found him, there is no need for further pictures in the mind. With that a change has taken place in the herdsman. He has seen the Bull, and is known by him; in that is the end of 'I'-solation.

Though all senses lead to the origin, listening is particularly referred to. The Great Bodhisattva Avalokitesvara (Kannon) awakened by hearing. Listen, wholly, totally! When not cut short by 'I', when there is no 'I' to interfere, the line is open. Outside and inside reflect each other. Sauntering along a valley, a Chinese Zen master told his pupil, 'Do you hear the murmuring brook? There is the entrance.'

Do we ever really just listen, open, whole-heartedly? What do we really hear, before I have already waded in and clamorously usurped the sounds? When the Buddha held up a flower, of all the big assembly only Kasyapa smiled; only he really saw.

Picture 4 – Catching the Bull

Once the Bull has been seen, he is known. The effort and courage spent has changed the herdsman, too, who has become used to seeing the Bull, and so, meeting the Bull suddenly head-on, he lays hands on him and catches him. The Bull can only be seen when he is around, if we bother or dare to look at the place where our own feet stand. Trying to see the Bull is missing the Bull. And trying to catch him is losing him; he can only be caught on impact.

This means conflict; the man and the Bull are not used to each other, cannot tolerate one another. The man must hang on as if for dear life. Only thus can he hold the Heart-bull fast! The Bull is wild and strong.

'Stubborn self-will rages in him and wild animal nature rules him'. Do we dare to even look at this Heart-bull? This is why he was so difficult to find; in cold blood, trying to, he cannot be seen – at best only his traces. Great honesty is necessary to tolerate the sight of him. To catch him at the point of collision is possible only by skill from the training and courage engendered on the way. A great change has taken place in the herdsman once he has caught the Bull.

Picture 5 – Gentling the Bull

With the Bull caught, the painful training begins. The Bull is wild and strong, used to his old ways and often still succeeds in running off, dragging the man with him, up the blue mountains of intellectual fancies, down the green valley of sensuality; shifting shapes, he tries to hide. The whip is needed; both man and Bull get exhausted.

But from the moment of recognition, of acknowledgement, a new process is at work which results in the catching, and makes possible the gentling of the wild Bull.

This is the conscious endurance of one's emotional reactions, without either being carried away by them or repressing them. In the beginning, to a man who has not yet caught the Bull, this seems impossible. The Bull is too strong; a glimpse and he has already escaped. But it is possible. There is a Middle Way between being carried away and fending off or repressing. This is to endure the presence of the Bull, enduring the conflict in willing awareness yet without being carried away. This restrains and gentles the Bull. During the training, man and Bull, I and the emotions, are in conflict – one pulls here, and the other there. Each fights, and each contributes; both come to understand their limits, and become familiar with each other. Thus both change.

The Bull, accustomed to the world of opposition of either this or that, wants to pull back to it. Profit and fame are still dear, if not material, then 'spiritual'. How far have I gone in my training? Or, disappointed, I don't seem to get any further! Of course I don't – I become less in this training, not more. Then I get frightened, or worry about losing the warm human touch; I can't lose it, having never had it – it is just the Bull lowing for his lush valleys. For his gentling, his curbing, for weaning him from his old lusts and rages, training is now essential, a wholehearted effort of handing oneself over to the restraints of the discipline. 'Always let the right thought persist' – and that is not easy when the Bull is fighting shy.

There are wild moments of opposition, of self-pity, and of resentment. Yes, here the whip is needed. They are a strange pair, the Bull and his herdsman. Both want and need to give in, yet both fight. But just in that they begin to come together. The taming, the gentling of the Bull is liberation from the Bull's animal nature; and that also means liberation from profit and fame, from attachment, including 'I'-attachment. Here the merging has its beginning.

Catching the Bull was difficult, but is easy compared with the tremendous task, the unremitting effort of truly gentling the Bull. And in every bout there is the ever-present danger of falling back into the old attitude of I doing the taming, in which man and Bull fly apart once more. For this a teacher is indispensable, for the Bull breaking loose at this stage turns perniciously deceptive. It is then the man who is caught, not the Bull. And the Bull is still wild, and wily!

Only when the Bull is truly gentled, when he has ceased to be what the Bull stands for, does the real change occur. That is the re-linking.

Picture 6 – Returning Home on the Back of the Bull

Here the struggle is now over. The seemingly impossible has taken place. The Bull's animal nature is changed, he is no longer a Bull, he and the herdsman are friends, mates. The Bull carries the man.

The emotional energy has sloughed off its compulsive aspect, has become humanized, once more friend and guide on the way home. The man, too, has lost his wilful separation, 'my way as it suits me', which is so typical of the little I whose other name is insecurity. In the beginning, I would ride the Bull – and this is why the Bull can run away with me. 'He who bestrides the tiger may not dismount'. The man who has laboured to gentle the Bull need not ride it; he may trust the Bull to carry him. It is the gentled Bull who knows the way home. No man knows that way – or we would have all gone it quite naturally! The man needs the gentled Bull – we have every reason to bestir ourselves to find and gentle our Heart-bull.

When the estrangement is over, the heart is fulfilled. Master Nansen used to teach, 'Heart is Buddha.' In time there arose attachment to that phrase, as there can still be attachment to the Bull; and so to help, making it quite clear, he changed his expression to, 'Neither Heart nor Buddha.'

Till Picture 6, the Bull was liable to run off, alone or with the man. What does this mean? Emotions are still able to erupt, invade the man, and carry him out of himself, back into the same old troubles, into violent conflicts outside and/or inside. He is not yet truly man but the shuttlecock of his emotions.

Training forces the acknowledgement of emotions when they arise along zones of individual weakness and take over. Training insists that the man consciously and willingly endures these emotional onslaughts and conflicts, that he does not shy away and try to avoid or refuse them. Strength develops in sustaining these onslaughts; as this bearing strength increases, the emotional energy loses its wild violence and itself becomes human. This change takes place in little shifts of attitude. Genuine insight is the result of such experiences, a becoming conscious of a change in one's habitual reaction-pattern. As that, it is possible by hindsight only, and is always accompanied by warmth of heart. Intellectual understanding alone falls short because in emotional conflicts conscious application cannot be sustained long enough without repression. This is why Buddhism stresses 'Right Effort', which is *not* I-intention to force an issue, but wholly, totally giving myself to the doing – in this case, to the suffering and enduring of the conflict, and that without ceasing to function smoothly in my everyday life and work.

To help this process, the training strongly insists on 'form'. If the man, the container of the energy, cannot keep his form, does not continue to function in his everyday life, the increasing conflicts (the fighting Bull) will shatter him. Untrammelled emotionality is debilitating and in the end destructive. Conversely there is in us an urge towards becoming whole which is possible only by gentling the Bull. It is he who knows the way home.

Till Picture 6 the Bull could still run away, back to the primitive pole of the energy scale, the animal or biological end which in the human realm is unbridled and destructive, but now, with the Bull carrying the man, a major shift has taken place – and with that a new danger emerges.

We are drawn to the Great or Heroic. Something shrills in us at hearing these words, the more so if our own life seems trivial, meaningless, a perpetual waiting for Life to happen. The small we disregard, brush away. What standards do we use to judge something as small, and who is the judge? Is it not because the small either does not stir me, leaves me cold? Or because I do not wish to be bothered and so conveniently judge what seems unimportant to me as small? 'Oh yes, easy, but not now, it does not suit me now and it does not matter.' Thus I can now ignore it in good conscience. What hypocrites we are. I seem to have a vested interest in not looking at the small things in my daily life, as if I feared something might be lurking underneath them. I do them automatically, robot-like, my mind occupied elsewhere. Thus I arbitrarily reject a good deal of my daily life, do not really live it. Then the unlived portion piles up against me as fear, threatening.

Should something 'Great' occur, I usually have no option. The 'Great' constellates the whole of me in a total effort and extracts a total reaction. It is the totality that subjectively, to me, makes the event not only great but also meaningful. I have lived it.

The training advocates the same total effort in all actions in one's daily life. The difficulty is that I cannot make that effort; I am far too weak, far too little. Nevertheless, I try to do so in the beginning, which is the reason why the Bull was so difficult to find. Total effort is going all out but in a special way, a total giving myself to and into it, unstintingly but without losing awareness. This distinguishes total giving in awareness from blind impulse, also total, but a compulsive, blind reaction in which the Bull has carried the man away. In the conscious giving oneself totally to what one is doing, even if 'only' washing up a cup, the Bull becomes cooperative. The Bull follows the man, and in that togetherness life takes on meaning and purpose. 'How wonderful, how miraculous, I carry wood and fetch water', as an old Zen master expressed it. The same applies to really laying something down; it is peculiarly difficult to really let go of something which emotionally entangles us; it nags at us all the time. Fitting here is the well-known story of a monk carrying a girl across a swollen ford; his companion, being upset by this, kept up a stream of complaints about the violation of the rules for monks. The first one kept quiet for a good while, but finally just quietly remarked, 'I put her down at the ford; why are you still carrying her?' We are amused by this and other such stories. Have we ever really pondered it? Do we not do the same? And don't we get hot in our defence, too?

The real laying down, the emotional liberation, giving up, letting go, presupposes that the Bull is tame, gentle. Having been given the robe and bowl of succession, the Sixth Patriarch of the Zen School was asked to leave the monastery. He was pursued and overtaken by a monk. Huineng, the story tells, laid down robe and bowl. We must ponder such stories carefully; they do not make historical reading, they are pointers. So he laid down what had been given, completely – bowl, robe, succession, his right to it, all that he had, was, and that was dear to him. He laid down himself, laid down his heart with what it hung on. This is to let go, when all has been laid down, no thing is left. Such laying down is quite different from giving in because I must, which is merely compulsion.

The pursuer, the story continues, made a grab for the robe and bowl but found he could not lift them up. All was laid down – and who could lift all? In the awe of this recognition and in the presence of that living, total situation, the pursuer was himself able to lay down his fierce desire and with a sudden inkling, humbly said, 'Elder brother, I did not come for robe and bowl; I came for the Dharma.' Yes, the total act constellates the other side. In Northern Buddhism this is doctrinally expressed by the helping hand of the Bodhisattva Kannon/Avalokitesvara. The difference between the primitive, biological pole of the energy and its spiritual pole is here clear. Both ends are suprapersonal; between them the energy slides unless it is humanized.

At that the Bull, gentled, humanized, carries the man home.

Picture 7 – Bull forgotten, Man Is.

This literal translation seems here preferable to the more usual one of 'Ox forgotten, Man remains'. Words can be harped on too much, but the Bull himself having become human, man is whole; only now really IS, lives his Being. What this Being is, words cannot reach; the picture points at it; the heart responds.

The human state was entered in the previous picture. 'Only from the human state is liberation from the Wheel possible.' With Picture 7 the specifically religious landscape opens.

The One Nature pervades everything. Only then, 'The heart rolls with the ten-thousand things; this rolling is truly mysterious.' Touch and response – this harmonious partaking in the living web of things, this effortless spontaneity, is the exact opposite of blind impulsiveness for which the beginner tends to mistake it.

Training disciplines are remarkably alike in all traditions; the human heart is the same under all our individual and cultural differences, and the way to its wholeness is the same for all. Nothing must be left out on this way, for the Bull, the primitive Adam, needs to be truly tempered and gentled, his very nature must have undergone transformation. Only then is the energy genuinely human. The work, the effort spent, is not only the condition for becoming whole, it is also an essential safeguard.

If the training was not thorough enough, if not enough bowing of the head and heart has taken place, if there was not a clear demarcation between man and Bull, and if both are not gentled sufficiently in the process, a wrong shift is liable to occur here. The Bull, forgotten, vanishes; but instead of the Bull being humanized, the man has now become a bull-man. Hence it is said, that from the side of man a real abdication of all he has achieved so far is needed. If he cannot lay it down, he becomes a bull-man. To avoid this calamity, the finer and finer probing of the training discipline is indispensable.

The human mind is a maker of pictures. Its other name is 'I'. If these pictures are infused by Bull energy, we are fatally prone to take them as true. Then it is my picture against yours, and we quarrel, fight, and suffer. This the Buddha saw clearly at his awakening. And so Buddhism, well aware of this basic fact, tends to 'describe' the inexpressible in terms of what it is not – and thus avoids the formation of pictures. In the early days of Buddhism being introduced to the West, this gave rise to the view that it is negative. It is not, it is supremely positive. A way that leads out of suffering surely ends in joy, and in a very specific form of it. This, too, the picture portrays. But the pilgrim must not settle here, cannot really settle here.

Of this training it is said that it cannot be done for oneself only. In the first stages it seems as if it had only to do with, I, my suffering, and the eradication of it. But as 'I' dwindles, the religious landscape opens in the absence of 'I'. Here a new dimension emerges, a new vector of growth and development which does not concern me but us, everything. With this, the head that looked at the shining glory in veneration, now bows, I abdicate. No-body enters the next stage.

The man has become whole; free of I, the split between I and the Bull is healed. And so is the split between I and other. He has become Man. The Fires no longer burn him. Having burnt away the root of I, in the absence of that fuel the energy is now sustaining as warmth and light. Wholly Man, he is not beyond anything. He shares in the sufferings common to our human lot; bearing his share in patience and gentleness, aware of the light that now shines in him, and shows him the way. He follows.

Picture 8 – Oblivion of Both Bull and Herdsman

An empty circle, complete not-ness. At the moment of death we go through it. 'I' fears death as the unknown, not knowable. All religions teach us to come to terms with this fear, to learn to die. But there is another death, the Great Death, that can be died alive, to Life. As a religious training, the Bull-herding analogy clearly shows this portal and points at something which no I can know or understand.

In the no-thing all opposites are resolved; not one, not two. The man, I as I know myself, dies, or goes into oblivion. Another impossibility is asked for this to take place: the form must be strong enough to hold. In utter darkness and oblivion are newly born the seeds of the spiritual man to come. To go into this circle is the real, final abdication, the letting go of oneself. Traditionally, it is described as a man hanging by one hand over a sheer cliff. Can he let go? The awesomeness might be symbolized in Christ's passion and crucifixion. From the Christian mystics we have the term 'Dark Night of the Soul' for it. Awesome, fearsome, dangerous, are correct words for describing this portal from the side of 'I'. As in everything, a danger lurks in it, a final test for him who enters without hope, who has and is nothing, to prove that he has truly entered the immovable spot, has died, become no-thing.

From Picture 7 onwards, the tamed energy strives inexorably towards the upper, the spiritual pole of its scale. If the form is not strong enough to contain its full potential, if the circle is not clearly delimited, the man, I, does not truly die but is carried away once more and suffers a seizure. One could also say that if the circle is not empty, if there is still a bit of something left, seizure will take place. Hence the Buddhist insistence on No-I: I must be dissolved to make room for a new centre. 'Tong Xuan (Entrance to the Deep Secret) – this mountain's summit is no place for ordinary folk.'

Master Hakuin calls this the Great Death. It is hinted at in such paradoxes as the Gateless Gate, or is called the Barrier of the Patriarchs. From the side of the trainee, it seems as if it had to be broken into. But as no 'I' can pass through, in the attempt to do so, with continuous effort spent, I myself get worn away. To No-I, the way is open.

To 'I', the last three pictures 8–10 are a mystery which no 'I' can understand. My attitude is therefore better one of awe and wonder, and the heart so touched will respond. To try to understand these last three pictures misses the target.

Picture 9 – The Return to the Ground and Origin

Through the empty portal the Great Death leads into the origin, back to the source. A restructuring takes place there, the rebirth of the true new man. He is in touch with all that is, the very centre of creativity from which the new emerges again and again, and this new is whole.

What the picture shows is the 'other shore', the nethermost region, from which the herdsman emerges, enriched, whole. Having passed through the portal of death, he is fearless, at one with all that is. This at-one-ment the picture portrays – the man is not even portrayed, so at one is he with what is. In this unfoldment the heart opens wide, its warmth flows.

Picture 10 – Entering the Market with Bliss-bestowing Hands

This new being, in warm relationship to all, has himself become the vehicle, the Way. He does not go 'beyond' – only I, deluded, can conceive a 'beyond'. He comes back to the market with bliss-bestowing hands. He is depicted large because he is whole. His heart has become sun-like. It shines from its own original nature. Thus it warms all.

With this, the Picture Series ends.

SUMMARY

There is a solidity in a 'man of Zen' that defies description. He sits loose, but cannot be pushed over. He is whole. However, this does not mean that he no longer cares about anything; the latter is an illusion of the little 'I' that always wants to be rid of problems and conflicts. The whole man cares very much, but does not make a personal problem out of it. He lives fully, and so death is not something to be afraid of. With the problem of death solved, most personal problems are solved, and there is only Life, the light, the strength and the warmth of it. This is what the bliss-bestowing hands point to. Of course, in the world there are all the pairs of opposites; there is light and dark, day and night. And there is joy and sorrow, happiness and pain, beauty and ugliness. No hands, however bliss-bestowing, can whisk away sorrow or pain; but at their touch, at the contact with a liberated heart full of love and understanding, anguish softens and ugliness is ameliorated. They lose their stranglehold, for that touch has the power to lift from the personal to the suprapersonal which is common to us all, and in which there is not only joy, but also the sorrow of things.

Of the Zen training it might be said that it liberates the man from both gods and demons that slumber in his own depth, who are not his but who on arising in him exact instant compliance. Something wholly other clings to them, a ghost-like, uncanny other-worldliness. Contact with that is the true religious experience. But if the form holds because it was trained to hold the full force at that impact, a seeing in awareness takes place. In the resulting restructuring, the forces I picture as gods and demons approximate human qualities, and man has become truly human. Thus of the Buddha it is said that he is the teacher of both men and gods; and he also redeemed the demons so that now they play a constructive role as guardians of the teaching. Is that, perhaps, why it is said doctrinally that from the Wheel of Being on which we whirl, liberation is possible only from the human state, when a man has become truly and totally human – and that everything rejoices at such an event? So it seems that we need to become truly human – not to lose ourselves in imaginary supermen and such like.

Thus human, there is a respect for, and sharing in gratitude with, all beings.

The question then is, how can such a way be walked? What is discipline? In effect, it is more an inner attitude; if for a few months to start with one takes one's daily life, just as it is, as one's religious discipline, things will begin to emerge. We live daily life anyway; we can put it to good use. To get up when it is time to get up, to do what is to be done, to go to bed. It sounds so simple – but, of course, we can't do it. Things irk us, or we want to shift things around as it suits us. So there is plenty of opportunity to react against the 'discipline'. These reactions are then accepted as part of oneself, and are willingly endured, 'suffered out', until their energy subsides.

The frequency of one's reactions under such a 'discipline' may at first surprise one; in fact, those reactions have always been there but we have long since learned to gloss over them, to hide from them, or to avoid situations that bring them out. Thus we have come to make a totally false 'picture' of ourselves. This self-image is worn away by the practice, leading to a new self-knowledge, with a concomitant influx of energy.

Such an attitude accepts whatever comes along. If it is something good, it is gratefully welcomed, enjoyed while it lasts, and not clung to when it goes. And something difficult is accepted as good practice: it, too, will pass. All this takes place while functioning smoothly in one's daily work and routine. And a daily hour is set aside to be by oneself, to ruminate or ponder, or just to slow down and learn to be quiet – but not be carried away into daydreaming.

As a practice, Zen accepts what comes – all is grist to its mill. Nothing is rejected, everything is made use of. And so one's life is lived fully; no unlived life piles up against one; and in living fully, one's daily life acquires meaning and purpose.

We can foster such an attitude, put our effort into living it. Little by little, we begin to change, and have thus started the great venture of finding and gentling the Bull. As a process, it is a long-term one.

Bodhidharma is said to have brought the Zen School from India to China. To him is attributed the saying that although all know the Way, very few walk it.

This Way starts in well-known territory. For this, a map and a guide are of great help; as C G Jung once remarked, to get lost on the highway in broad daylight is merely frustrating. It is on this known stretch of the way that the wayfarer needs maps, and acquires the skill and the strength to venture forth alone when the known path has come to an end.

Chapter Five

The Analytical Psychology of C G Jung

THE PREVIOUS CHAPTER described the training analogy of the Bull-herding Pictures. But as one can get too engrossed with one picture, it might be useful to have a look at another portrayal of the Herdsman I and the Heart-bull energy. For this, the psychology of C G Jung is the best representation, and it has the further advantage of being a Western one, with facets peculiar to us Westerners.

It is, of course, impossible to set out the whole of it in a short chapter. Those interested will find 'An Introduction to the Psychology of C G Jung' by Frieda Fordham a good introduction, and indeed a helpful exposition for certain difficulties in the training. But what we are concerned with here is how energy is conceived in Jungian psychology and whether this helps us to become more aware of some familiar – and not so familiar – facets of it in ourselves.

What Jung calls the Psyche, the enlivening, life-giving principle, bears certain features of the soul but in a non-Christian, pre-Christian connotation – like the Latin word 'anima', that which animates, makes alive, makes live. In itself, a principle is a concept, but is experienced as tremendous force – as when in spring we see the first crocus leaves spear through the half-frozen ground and our hearts are touched with awe and wonder at what gives those soft blades their penetrating strength.

Jung calls this strength or force in us humans Psychic Energy, thus distinguishing it from physical energy. Though both interact, the former is the strength or energy of the Heart-bull. What is at stake in the training is the transformation of this energy from its elemental or primitive aspect through humanization to its spiritual pole. The Bull-herding Pictures portray the stages of this transformation. Jungian psychology also seems to advocate this transformation, but uses a picture series, the Archetypes, which Jung found to be innate in us anyway. He calls the process Individuation, becoming aware of the totality in oneself, hence leading from the narrow 'I'-perception to what he calls the Self.

For this reason, we are here not overly concerned with introvert and extrovert, or the four functions of conscious perception, that is, thinking, feeling, sensation and intuition. Our interest is in I, the focus as it were of consciousness, and in the energy.

Jung sees the household of the Psyche in three layers – Consciousness with I being its apex, the Personal Unconscious beneath it, and finally the depth of the Collective Unconscious with its tremendous store of energy, not accessible to I in cold blood.

I am not consciousness as such. I cannot consciously hold too much in my mind. I cannot at the same time concentrate equally on the book I read and the music I hear, or correctly and efficiently add up a column of figures while deciding where to go for my holiday. I cannot think out two quite unrelated problems at the same time. Like a searchlight, I can focus at what I have in mind by an act of will, directing the spotlight at the content, leaving other areas in the dark. I can recall things to mind by shifting the spotlight. But as we all know, recall of memory is not complete, and not always possible at will.

Since I can only know what I have become conscious of, and because I can usually recall things and events by shifting the spotlight or focus of consciousness, this faculty gives me the notion of I, a seeming entity. And as I am not conscious of anything else, I consider myself the sole agent of my actions, their motivator.

That is a fond illusion we know to our cost, for we cannot always recall what we want, when we want, or do what we have in mind. Something else in us intervenes and obstructs our decided plan of action. We also forget things, not temporarily but past recall.

What we have forgotten has receded beyond the beam of the searchlight, though it was once within its beam. This area Jung calls the Personal Unconscious. Littered with things forgotten, of too low impact to be retained in consciousness, and with things we would rather forget as too painful, lowering, shameful, etc.; it also contains all the many things subliminally noted but of too little interest to be consciously taken note of and retained. But it is a grave mistake to consider it just a lumber room; not only do its contents influence my thinking and actions, but to it belong two functions, one mediating to consciousness, the other to the Collective Unconscious, respectively the Persona and the Shadow. Within the reach of what is familiar to us, we can conceive of the Personal Unconscious as follows. Though my eyes saw the woman with the black hat who passed me yesterday at the bus stop, I did not register this sense-impression because my mind was otherwise engaged. I remained unconscious of it – yet another part of which I am unconscious, registered it, and is capable of producing the impression if suitably stimulated. Or, if I am really absorbed in a book which fascinates me, I will not consciously hear my name when called unless I am shouted at, though at other times I may complain about my lack of concentration.

As to the two functions of the Personal Unconscious, the first is to an extent familiar. In my job or profession, a certain mode of behaviour is expected of me over and above my professional skill. This – it not being really me – I don, like a nurse her uniform, as an appropriate mask, the actor playing his role. This professional mask conveniently covers my human traits which do not correspond to the role I am expected to play. This kind of play-acting is convenient because it facilitates professional relationships, and depersonalizes the actor. Certain qualities are expected of, say, a clergyman, and he is bound by appropriate behaviour, at least in public. And since he can be trusted to sustain his role, appropriate relationships can be established.

Good manners, right behaviour, etc., would seem to fall into this aspect. They, too, facilitate relationships, together with trustworthiness or sustaining the form, cooperation and consideration. Is that perhaps why, with our loss of cultural values, good manners, etc., we talk so much and longingly about communication and relation? Or is it perhaps because having nothing else, my 'I' sits on me like a ton of bricks and in order to lose it I want to pour myself into the other? But my naked features are so unprepossessing that I had better dress up as the occasion demands rather than expecting you to unburden me of them – the more so when you expect me to do the same for you. How can that further relation? It rather alienates.

It is the Persona which makes it possible to establish correct relations and human cooperation. But its danger is that I rather like my performance and the licence it gives me, and so am tempted to keep the mask, mistake myself for the mask, believe it to be me. A doctor leaves his white coat in the surgery and steps out, the human being that he is. He does not keep it on in the family circle, or go to bed with it!

Thus the Persona, useful if not essential for its purpose, can be misused as a cover for my weaknesses and so needs careful handling, that is, taking if off when not needed. As a smoke screen, it has connections with what I would rather not be conscious of – with the next layer of the Personal Unconscious, the Shadow.

Though to think of layers is useful in conceptualizing, there are no sharp limits, and not only do the boundaries blur with increasing depth, but the merging shapes shift or erupt upwards. The more unacquainted we are with ourselves (or the more dishonest), the more crowded and compelling the picture-show. Acquaintance with the forces at work within us thins their delusory play.

The constellation that best portrays the next layer of the Personal Unconscious, but also mediates approach to the powerhouse of the Collective Unconscious and is partly contaminated by it, Jung calls the Shadow.

I like to be conscious of my good qualities. My not so nice ones I may be aware of, but prefer not to think of them. What reminds me of them, I relegate to limbo. But those which I truly despise and fear, I can only see in others and am sure of not having them at all. But it is just these which complement my 'good' image and make up my shadow. Because I despise and deny these qualities in me, I become infuriated beyond reason if somebody else exhibits them in my presence.

This is further exacerbated by the Shadow being loaded with collective content of evil – not mine, but ours – for which the devil is an apt symbol. Much of the terror that the Shadow has for us consists of the contamination of my unpleasant and nasty traits with the collective content which is not mine.

Underneath the Personal is the Collective Unconscious. Though its structure, too, is conceived of in layers, there is interaction between them, one shifting into the other, or affecting the other. It is timeless.

Perhaps the best model for the Psyche is a cone of which I, the focus and searchlight of consciousness, am the apex. The beam that I think I direct but in fact am, can penetrate down to a certain extent, just as far as my own empirical experience or my memory reaches. Memory can also trick me because in this twilight zone it may enter a variety of combinations. Beyond that reach, for me, there is darkness. Since the light is me, an ephemeral manifestation, it constitutes only the veriest top of the cone of human experience and indeed of life experience. I do not consciously know how my nails grow, cannot consciously, that is by an act of will, grow my hair. Yet, grow they do; I do not know how or why.

About the Collective Unconscious, nothing concrete can be said because it is unconscious, not known, and inconceivable. It seems a kind of powerhouse. Certain grave and constant effects of it have been observed, functions of energy which Jung calls Psychic Energy, the non-physical aspect of life energy that enlivens, forms and makes life, animates forms, and recedes again in death, leaving a corpse.

Since we are born human, programmed human as it were, we perceive this energy, its functioning in us, and compelling us to action, in specifically human pictures. And because these pictures, in order to be compelling, must carry a very high energy potential, the attributes of fascination, irresistibility, omnipotence, other-worldliness, the totally other, or godlike, even divinity, cling to them, as well as awe and fear.

And so, approaching the Collective Unconscious, which underlies the reach of our searchlight, the first power nodule we meet at its portal is the despised and feared Shadow, that figure or picture that for an individual is the sum total of all his unacknowledged and unknown but feared weaknesses, inadequacies, wickedness, deceitfulness, shameful lusts, pettiness, meanness, domineering itch, etc.

Thus in Jungian psychology, any approach to the Unconscious starts, and must start, with the integration of the personal Shadow, our conscious awareness of it – and so also delineation of or discrimination from the collective Shadow which cannot be assimilated as it is not mine. Just this differentiation breaks the undeniable power that the Shadow has over us because by means of it our personal share becomes known and thus subject to alteration. So this energy nodule is disentangled by our acceptance of the personal part of the Shadow figure. But because this dents our dear self-image, our resentment against this process is great indeed and constitutes very real suffering, the more so as its collective component is also loaded with fear and terror – as our dreams reveal.

Dreams, in Jungian psychology, are seen as mediators, the language in which the Collective Unconscious attempts to communicate with us, the younger, conscious part. Of course, the delineation between Consciousness and the Collective Unconscious is not sharp anyway, and we do have the propensity to sink back into it at times, and need to do so in sleep. Consciousness and the Collective Unconscious form the totality of the Psyche, our inner entity, an ontogenetic phylogenetic compound corresponding to our physical entity. The Collective Unconscious is thus conceived of as immensely old, and the modern language of the cerebral conscious part of the individual is unknown to it. It uses the old picture language which is so difficult for us to decode – but vital to do so as its human experience far outdistances individual experience; moreover it complements it and so can act as a correcting function to our wayward, one-sided consciousness. The developmental, 'wholemaking' approach of Jungian psychology proceeds through the integration of unconscious contents towards Individuation. For this it is necessary to learn the language of the Collective Unconscious.

We dream every night – whether we remember our dreams or not. Modern research has found that if we are deprived of our dream periods which are part but not all of our sleeping time, we begin to show stress symptoms. It is as though we need to be recharged by periodic returns to the 'Mother', though we are unaware of this in our conscious 'I'-activities. If these 'I'-activities deviate too far from our totality, the Collective Unconscious seems to attempt to restore the balance via dreams. Dreams are the language it knows and sleep is the time when it can speak.

Dream interpretation has played a major role in all cultures from primitive times, but it is less accessible to our differentiated modern consciousness. Yet we all know what nightmares are, for we all have them. And it is a rare person who cannot remember at least one dream so loaded (the energy potential of the dream) that it impresses itself on waking consciousness with never-to-be-forgotten intensity.

Thus the Collective Unconscious is conceived in Jungian psychology as a matrix, the psychic component of the phylogenetic substrate in which are furled up all future possibilities, a potential to be realized, unfolded, and manifested in living it by the individual who makes the effort to do so. The so-called correcting function of the Collective Unconscious must not be misunderstood in the sense of a conscious attempt, but is best conceived of as an innate, natural reaction against excessive imbalance or one-sidedness. Excessive one-sidedness has always ended in extinction; harmony, balancing – outer and inner – is a law of nature which operates impartially.

The Collective Unconscious can exert this correcting function from the point of the total or whole individual, attempting to point out, as it were, the undeveloped components which are needful, and checking excesses. It is aptly named 'collective' for it is not the possession of one individual; all share in it, and as such it also points towards the future. Trends towards new orientations, especially in times of disorientation and change, are urged by the unconscious, and it depends on the individual interpretation, perhaps on the readiness and preparedness of the individual, how he expresses or formulates such promptings. In primitive societies, it was a major function to interpret 'big dreams' correctly as they concerned the weal and woe of the community, not only of the individual.

It goes without saying, then as now, that these interpretations need to be in the language of the time, fitting the state of consciousness (inside) and circumstances (outside). The difficulty is to find correct expressions rather than to regress to well worn but out-dated symbols – as war-propaganda and religious fanaticism invariably bring up the same old things. This applies also on the individual level, as when one's neighbour suddenly seems to take on the features of the devil, or one's love those of a goddess.

This process Jung calls Projection, when symbolic pictures are projected onto persons, ideas, or any '-ism'. Because of the high-energy component, a tremendous vitality and fascination cling to them, and they are hard to see through and dissolve.

Projections happen to me; I do not make them – indeed, I cannot make them. I fall in love, or out of it. Try as I may, I can- not make myself do so. It happens, or it does not. There is no halfway stage; nor is there any reason. In that lies the danger; in a state when a dazzling radiance has taken pos-session of me, I can do things I could never contemplate or countenance in cold blood. The atrocities of fanaticism, excesses that far outreach any reasonable actions, are all too well known.

However, projections occur not only of such symbolic pictures, of archetypical images that carry all the collective energy. These, just because of their tremendous energy, tend to burn themselves out – or they burn out their host. Of less high-energy content, but in the long run perhaps just as perni-cious, are the ordinary or personal projections. Our daily life swarms with this type. 'To the pure, everything is pure.' All that I am myself I naively impute also to my fellow beings. If I am myself devious, I mistrust you. The more direct you are, the more I suspect you of hidden motives and will go to any length to circumvent you – thus ruining what otherwise could be a very harmonious relationship.

The main difference between the so-called normal person and the so-called neurotic is that the former conveniently distributes pleasant projections within the immediate circle of family and friends, and outside that charmed circle, over the fence or border, or in nebulous 'bodies' like establishment or some '-ism', dwell the nasty ones. The so-called neurotic is less skilful in the distribution, lacks the strength to keep them outside, and so they invade the family circle.

Perhaps a variation of this type of projection is our propensity for wishful thinking when I do not really hear what you say but only hear what I wish, or interpret what you say as I wish – and then blame you bitterly.

To distinguish between personal and archetypal projections, the latter are perceived as fateful or fated. Their high energy content make for this irresistible fascination which imbues the most banal commonplace things with dazzling radiance. Both types estrange the individual from his environment and make any real relationship impossible.

Not having made them, I cannot dissolve projections; at best I can with much difficulty dislodge them from their carrier-object, or they fall off it themselves, usually a rather shattering experience as we all know when we happen to fall out of love. But that neither diminishes nor changes the energy content that now strives to find another carrier. Dissolution of the projecting urge of the energy is a long and painful labour which entails that the projected contents are recognized as pictures and their energy as belonging to the household of the Psyche – not the quality of the carrier.

Nodule points of the Collective Unconscious, the energy functions that go into gear for the experiences or situations that are grave and constant in human experience, Jung has called Archetypes.

Whereas Jungian terms like 'extrovert' and 'introvert', and 'complex', have long since become familiar even in ordinary language, the concept of Archetypes seems to present a real difficulty. It need not. Though this term is extremely fitting in one way, in another it is misleading in seemingly denoting a 'thing'. In his earlier writings Jung referred to Archetypes as Dominant Functions of Images of the Collective Unconscious. This is helpful, for a function is not a thing; and if we keep in mind that the Collective Unconscious is the powerhouse of life energy, then it is not too difficult to conceive of the Archetypes as functions of this energy within the human framework of experience and perception – but different from that of, say, a duck.

Ducklings hatched out by a hen and adopting her instantly as mother to be obeyed and followed, will on encountering water naturally take to it in spite of the frantic protests of the hen. How do they know? To say, 'the inborn collective image', merely begs the question. Perhaps better expressed, when encountering such an image which is the collective experience of all water birds, an energy-function is triggered off which is of such overwhelming power that it forces instant response. In the case of the ducklings, the forced response is that of a water bird or duck, and not that of a hen, which would drown. So these energy functions compel the individual to action concordant with its species. Thus they could be seen as life-guides. It goes without saying that here only a very rough sketch is given.

The animal has no option; it obeys. If hunger stirs, it becomes restless and is forced to seek food. Self-protection and defence is compulsive, governed by often elaborate rituals of threat, effective at a certain distance. Though usually protectors of the individual, two of these functions might be called supra-personal as they guard the continuation of the species, if need be against the interest of the individual: reproduction and care of the young. Hence the short mating season during which the usual self-protective instincts are at a minimum, and aggression between competitors is violent. The young are born in season, are cared for, and have various forms of licence not tolerated in the adult.

The overcoming of the self-protective by the supra-personal instincts, and reversal to the norm, or one, say hunger, being relieved, another, say tiredness after the labour of the procurement of food, takes over, is known as instinct-crossing. In the animal, this takes place of itself, and ensures that none of these tremendous energies can go wild, go their whole length as it were, which would inevitably result in destruction and catastrophe.

With us human beings, and perhaps as a result of our becoming conscious, that is self-conscious, it is as if we had lost these reliable guides. My desires, wants, appetites, rejections, have become unbridled, far exceeding what is needful. We pride ourselves on our much valued free will, without realizing that it amounts to little unless infused from underneath by just this energy, which usually goes unsuspected. More fatally, however, with the loss of that precious instinct-crossing, we have irrevocably been expelled from the Garden of Eden. We have no mating season; our appetites, lusts and aggressions are unbridled. Thus from the earliest times we have had recourse to systems of behaviour to combat them. Whether those systems were tribally, religiously or socially expressed and enforced, they had to be kept at the threat of terrible punishments, and yet we always have been peculiarly unable to keep them even if rationally wishing to do so. 'Needs must when the devil drives' and thus they work havoc.

These dominant forces, compelling, numinous, irresistible in their pristine or primordial function, Jung called the Archetypes. What an Archetype is we cannot know. They occur to us only in picture language, direct in dreams, or in projection. We may experience these images as fateful, but they are not the Archetype, not the energy function itself. Again as analogy, water appears to the duckling and forces the innate response. There are also 'learned' responses for which the picture is even more important.

The insecure and lonely position of the human 'I' might be the direct result of alienation from this primal energy and its images. What are these images for us human beings? Surely, they are concerned with what is grave and constant in human experience: father/mother, mate, child; changes like threshold crossings of birth, puberty, marriage, death; states of helplessness, betrayal, danger, need, succour; the bliss of alleviation. These are perennial; and there are perennial answers to them, which have informed us and can inform us still if we are but willing to learn, willing to listen again.

Jungian psychology thus can help the individual to a widening out of the narrow horizon of 'I' and towards a re-linking with the enlivening forces of the Collective Unconscious by conscious experience of them. Both the conscious situation in daily life, and dreams, are made use of in this process. Jung continuously stresses the importance of the very difficult task of becoming aware of the Shadow, which is the portal to the deeper layers of the Collective Unconscious. Without such differentiation, infantile and primitive traits in the personality will inevitably be shied away from and repressed, thus tainting and distorting the inner and outer life. What is not acknowledged and accepted inside, projects itself outside as if the rejected or unacknowledged component were staging a self-representation so that it may be perceived and restored, lived. Life strives towards wholeness, and needs to be lived, not necessarily in acting out, for example, a violent trait, but in the awareness of its existence and the strength of containing it consciously, suffering it without letting rip. Because of its high energy potential, this means an endurance, a very real suffering or 'passion', which is precisely what the transforming agent is. Not a sublimation, rather the energy is being transformed, humanized.

Thus it is possible for the deeper layers of the Collective Unconscious to emerge, and to become perceptible as inner qualities and functions, rather than the dazzling fascination of projections where willy-nilly the carrier is mistaken for the projection.

Jung repeatedly says that the concept of the Shadow is not difficult to grasp intellectually, though desperately difficult and painful to really live through its experience. Contrary to this, the next deeper layer, anima/animus, as they appear respectively in man and woman, or the contra-sexual function, poses enormous difficulties even for its conception. However, this need not be so if the contra-sexual aspect is kept in mind. If one falls in love, the beloved takes on the features of a god or goddess – perceived by the lover; whereas loving a person, however deeply, the weakness and strength, the good and not so good traits, are seen and loved equally. But having fallen in love, no weaknesses can be perceived – gods have none. And if the fact rushes home eventually that such a god or goddess has feet of clay, there is violent resistance and/or shattering disillusionment. This need not be with persons only, as history shows, but here we stay with the personal. Since we mix up love and sex, the anima/animus images are conceived, if at all, too personally, as 'love-pictures'. They are not; and the contrasexual aspect, taken as such, warns of that mistake. For with them we are in the realm of the gods. Though there is a goddess of love, she is but one differentiation, one function, derived much later with developing human consciousness, of The Goddess, who is mother, matrix, womb, and world, who brings forth all that is. The god of love, too, is such a differentiated function of The God, father and fertilizer, power and spirit.

Thus the contra-sexual images at root lead back – via the parents, to the cosmogonic parental pair, the numinous figures and blinding light of the religious experience, who have succoured and strengthened us human beings through the ages. These, Jung calls respectively the Great Old Woman and the Wise Old Man – rightly so, for this is how they appear when their energy is realized. Their perception gives meaning and relatedness to the individual life. Only then can a unifying factor emerge, the Self, which is now seen as the core of the personality and to which I, the ego, am related as a part of the whole. This new centre is in itself a totality, but relates to all that is. With that, the alienation, the lack of identity and fear which are the bane of mere I-existence have ended, and the whole individual, as a conscious carrier of life, takes his place in the community, with his creative powers released and with the strength to apply them.

Thus in the Collective Unconscious slumbers a component for future development which urges towards realization. We are all born human, with a longing or yearning towards something; we do not know what, but usually find some picture for it. Perhaps most neutrally expressed, it is to find out the meaning of ourselves in the world we find ourselves in. Due to our consciousness it might be possible that in us this process of coming into being, of changing forms, of development and evolution obeying inherent laws unawares, could become conscious of itself.

Every individual feels this potential, this urge. Every 'I' feels itself both tiny and immense. But since I am just the conscious top of this immensity, ephemeral as such, the fatal mistake is for 'I' to try to appropriate what is Not-I, which invariably bursts the seams of 'I' while retaining the short-sightedness of the individual 'I', together with the blind compulsion of the unconscious and its pictures. What is necessary is a shift of attitude: to stand firmly in human individuality, humbly aware of one's human limitations but not shifting from the human qualities in face of this immensity; and by that rendering it human, so that it can manifest in human qualities, almost lending it human eyes to look out through them, and to see, perceive, and reflect what is seen.

This shift, in Jungian psychology, is called variously, the integration of the personality, Individuation, or the shift of the focal point from 'I' to Self. In Buddhism it is simply called awakening, as from the narrow dream of 'I'-ness.

With that is restored to the individual his birthright which was lost in the tremendous struggle of becoming conscious. This is a process which is not yet ended, but seems to have got stuck at a halfway stage of perceiving only the veriest top of all, myself. Thus our awkward self-consciousness which is so crippling in all performance, because it is so little.

When we can see what we really are, we have entered our parents' house (not just our father's) which has many mansions and because it is familiar, we can move freely and spontaneously in it, respecting all, and living 'happily ever after' in accord and relationship with our family. With that is also restored the sense of awe and wonder, of reverence and joy, of conscious participation in what is coming to be within our sphere of action. Thus the heart is content because there is meaning and purpose in our individual, ephemeral life. And because the totality is seen, not I, but it sees through this ephemeral form and is conscious of itself. With that the old fear of death is also transcended, and so is all enmity. What remains is warmth or relationship to all that is without and within, and the understanding of it in reverence.

Needless to say, the full development, Individuation, is indeed a very rare event. In this discussion, only the developmental part of the psychology of C G Jung has been considered as relevant for our theme.

Chapter Six

Round About

THE SPIRITUAL WAY is a pilgrimage rather than a sight-seeing tour. So it is best undertaken for the love of it rather than for what I can get out of it. Then it will prosper.

This our theme winds itself as around a mountain. And just as a mountain looks different when seen from different directions, so our theme sometimes repeats itself, sometimes seemingly contradicts itself, or again opens up new vistas. The mountain is the same; but unless I have been all the way around it, my view of it is partial, one-sided only. Used to its soaring north flank, how will I recognize the mountain when facing its gentle southern slope – or vice versa? But once I have been around it, got its shape, I will recognize it from all angles. Repeating what is already familiar, presenting new aspects, correcting some and filling in other details, the whole may begin to reveal itself to the circumambulating pilgrim.

Though change is the hallmark of all being, in our time change around us seems to have taken on speed at such a rate that all traditional frameworks have broken down. We are out of breath, cannot keep step, lag behind more and more, bombarded by outside knowledge like the staccato commentary of a sports reporter – the advances of nuclear technology, the digital revolution, etc. Yet the majority of us still cling to a mechanical world-model which no longer fits our time. Becoming ever more disorientated, alienated from our time and from ourselves, we look around for some answer, any answer – and because the pressure is great, become ever more one-sided and/or gullible.

In such perplexity, might it not prove instructive to cease from too much outside striving and rather go on an inner 'walkabout', an inner pilgrimage which can acquaint us with the different, even opposing aspects of the same mountain? In the last two chapters we considered the Zen training analogy of gentling the Bull, and the Analytical Psychology of C G Jung. How can two such seemingly disparate aspects as the two discussed serve to regain orientation in our normal, everyday world and within ourselves? And how can they help us on our way around the mountain and up to it – if we feel so inclined? Perhaps because both show, in their very different formulations, the same obstacles, the same necessary steps in the beginning. They also show that though outward circumstances have changed enormously during the last millennium, man himself has changed little if at all. The same wilfulness, cravings, lusts and urges hold sway, and in the absence of any cultural values, result in untrammelled egoity which is as contagious and destructive as any virulent disease.

Thus the cause of our problems is always seen as lodged in 'the other' side, 'other than I', that is, away from me who is good. Our world is split because we are split. And just as to the pure everything is pure, to the split everything is divided – us and them, East and West, communism and capitalism, establishment and underground, children and parents, etc. The cause, the fault is never seen as lodged in myself. Yet the world, I, we all are split into two warring halves; and this split cannot be healed from the outside, not by legislation or commandments. It can only be healed in the individual. The ball is therefore in the court of the individual, me, and, it is for me to make a start to contain these two warring halves, suffering them in the living body rather than in abstract ideas of my mind.

Concretely, this means that I have to suffer the presence of the despised other, my resistances, dislikes, fears – in short the proximity of all that is incompatible with me. I have to endure its presence in me without giving way to it, without being carried away by it. This is the great effort that our time needs for the liberation of the hidden springs of life, for the quickening of the individual.

Societies are made up of individuals, not of ciphers to which we seem to be reduced. It is not our society that is wrong, but we, the individuals who make it up; we are very ill indeed. 'If the cart sticks in the mire, will you whip the cart or the ox?'

Thus far, there is complete agreement between the Jungian stress on the integration of the Shadow, and the Daily Life Practice in Zen training which is geared to bring up all the weaknesses and inadequacies inherent in the individual, lopsided me. The danger in the Jungian system is that it may be kept discursive only, on the mental level, leaving out the physical aspect, the very real suffering which working with the emotions entails. And the danger in Zen training is that in a very subtle shift I, who need to suffer the proximity of the emotional energy, side step and precariously attempt to nevertheless keep control. I thus evade the full impact of the energy and the ensuing conflict, start arguing and questioning about it instead of enduring its presence. Careful guidance and supervision is necessary for both, but the stress on the physical side of the practice gives Zen training a practical angle and gauge.

In all religious training, strength for sustained effort needs to be available. In Zen training this effort is expressed in Buddhist terminology as 'right effort'. It implies that not I do it with my will and strength, but that I hand myself wholly into the doing, or as wholly as I can, yet remaining with it, not blindly 'doing'. A person suffering from lack of just that energy is in need of psychological adjustment. Any attempt at religious training – as distinct from the support and succour of religious observances which may indeed 'right' him – remains futile, may even end in catastrophe. This warning cannot be stressed too much. In his writings, C G Jung makes the same point. He differentiates sharply between adaptation and individuation, and warns against attempts at the latter unless the whole personality demands it for its unfoldment.

After that, the two ways part. The Jungian goes into the emotional involvements of anima/animus, moods and opinions, and proceeds, ideally, via the archetypal parental pair to the shift from 'I' to Self, the full identity to which 'I' is subservient.

Zen training seems to take another road. With the Daily Life Practice is coupled a meditative practice which, when established, makes use of a theme as a conducive handle to throw the now experienced practiser into his full identity, into contact with his ground of being and source of life. After that it insists on the long training through differentiations clearly perceived into aware alignment with the ground of being.

The difficulty with words like 'awareness' is that they seem to presuppose a subject, I, who by the act of observation becomes aware or conscious of something. This has led to a false sense of supremacy of I, the cerebral, conscious part only, a kind of insecurely balanced commentator jealously defending his uneasy position. But it is the other way round. As an experiment: think of something in a very concentrated way, and give yourself a strongish pinch in the soft flesh of your arm. Awareness comes rushing to the point of impact – I do not have to consciously think of it, it hits me; I am the recipient rather than the agent. This immediate, instant awareness that acts on me is both direct and total. 'Aware alignment' referred to above is meant in this sense. An untrained 'I' finds this difficult to understand, for naturally I feel that awareness ought to be mine and want it to be mine, thus totally missing the point. I cannot have it ever.

Which religious way to choose for the inner pilgrimage is today the choice of the individual. The one he feels drawn to, to which his whole heart inclines after careful pondering and circumambulation, is perhaps the best for him. This choice is important because the traditional symbols and values of the indigenous tradition have in the main lost their attraction. And unless the heart inclines, there is not enough strength available to continue when the going becomes rough, as inevitably it will. But it must stand to reason, must make sense to a certain degree. Blind practice is not likely to lead to clear seeing. Nor is blind infatuation with some new, trendy, 'instant' method a likely way. Ours is an irreligious age. Jung says rightly that the altar where once the spirit was throned now stands empty. And since nature abhors a vacuum, we are very prone to install false gods on that empty altar, any fad or 'ism' that catches our fancy and promises quick returns. So we rush to collect the goodies and complain afterwards that we were deceived. Who deceived me? My folly, mistaking the inner pilgrimage for a bargain sale!

Though the Jungian way in its developmental aspect attempts the same, it is not yet forged into a traditional way. In his later writings, Jung points towards it, but in its present form as a system, the religious dimension is missing. Perhaps, and most certainly not in a destructive sense, it might provisionally be said that the Jungian way can lead to a state approximating that which is described in pictures 6 and 7 of the Bull-herding analogy. This appears all the more so as Jung himself seems to have gone further along that way – and the remarkable, the quite unprecedented achievement of this great man is that he walked it unaided, by himself, and so clear-eyed, so humbly that he missed nothing, and could leave an immense and well-documented literature behind, establishing a way along which others could train and which his school continues. If this way became a bit watered down, like ripples flattening out in a pond, it is rather proof that the great old man was so far ahead of his time that it is difficult indeed to keep step with him. Thus it seems extremely useful to refer again and again to his own writings, learning to read them in his sense. How his way will develop further is not yet known. It certainly points to, and could lead into, the spiritual realm; whether this will be followed, is not yet known either. The possibilities are there.

With Picture 7 of the Bull-herding analogy of Zen training, the religious sphere is approached, reaches its culmination in Picture 8, the Great Death, and when the new alignment, or perhaps better realignment, has taken place, it swings back to the human realm in Picture 10, the way of descent in compassionate understanding to hold out a helping hand with a big reassuring smile.

What does the pilgrimage round about the mountain reveal? In the Buddhist formulation of change, there is the steady swing or rhythm of 'coming to be, ceasing to be', of birth and death, creation and destruction. Both are in us, too. To approach wholeness we must not avoid opposites, cling to one and detest the other. The soaring flank and the gentle slope are both the same mountain. That is the 'round' or full view. Meanwhile, we are partial, one-sided, side with this or that. And so there are those who see predominantly something more than I, greater, better, whatever, and set out to follow it in an adventurous yet humble spirit. And there are those, who, on perception of just that more than I, feel at once that it must be for me and try to bring it down to my level, thus destroying it. There are universal warnings against the latter – Pandora's box, a Japanese fairy tale (Urashima Taro), and a very beautiful rendering in an African tale told by Laurens van der Post in 'The Heart of the Hunter'. The latter, abbreviated, is the story of a 'sky-woman' trapped by and happily married to a herdsman. She possessed a basket which the husband had promised never to look into. But his curiosity grew and one day the inevitable happened and he looked. The basket was empty – to him. Upon which the woman vanished.

It is a well-known motif. The Chinese classic, Daodejing, has as its second sentence, 'The name that can be pronounced is not the real name'. When the unknown becomes known, it loses meaning and becomes empty, nothing. This is vulgarization, empty understanding in which the real 'content', that enlivening yet elusive something which is the heart is lost. Then, what remains is 'nothing but ...'.

Today, who can deny it, the world suffers from a thousand ills. There is nothing that gives restraint to unbridled egoity. The great religions have by and large lost the congregation of their faithful, and it seems that we are growing out of the age of those great religions into an empty 'nothing but ...', only too prone to substitute a lesser value for the one lost. But with that we have also lost the restraining and succouring functions which are embedded in religion. In consequence, we are dreadfully naked, alone and insecure – liable of being invaded by any fancy or frenzy as well as of being overcome by our lusts and drives, and quite unbeknown to ourselves have become their slaves. The faith that can move mountains as well as keep us in bounds and give place and meaning to an individual life, to shield it from inner uprushes, is not something that I can inculcate at will.

And so it seems that two things are of utmost importance today: a courageous acquaintance with the very real forces within us, for which the Jungian way is extremely helpful; and a decoded but reasonably correct interpretation of the true function of religion as such but which does not empty it of its inherent content. What is necessary from our side is not attempts at empty explanations, but to bestir ourselves to re-collect and re-discover what has become scattered and forgotten yet is the *sine qua non* to still the heart's longing: to become fully aware of our human state and thus fully human, a whole being, acting as such always and everywhere. There is a crying need for this, and for at least a few who can set an example and who less by word than by their whole being can show the way. Among mountains, there is always one which is the highest peak and a few other giants of nearly the same stature, but all, the highest and the lowest, are mountains. Among us human beings the great beacons of a Buddha or a Christ stand out over millennia, but there is also a chain of giants that hand on the torch as it were; and we ordinary people can also be fully human without reaching the great peaks of *homo religious.*

This seems to be the true task, the beckoning adventure of our time, more arduous even than space travel, and subject to the same risks. Societies are not entities on their own, they are made up of us human beings. If there were human beings with deeper humanity, greater humanness – not because that is their ideal which they rarely approximate but simply because they are – who can deny that the world we live in would of itself also have become better?

But the road towards it is steep and exacting. Truly, I am my own obstacle. I cannot overcome myself by an act of will without refusing, rejecting and thus losing something. Fullness, wholeness, however, is inclusive; moreover, it is a totality which is both more and other than the separate parts. Thus the growth towards wholeness does not exclude anything but rather is a process of suffering the hitherto excluded, rejected parts to draw near and to endure their presence without being overwhelmed by them. This re-collecting, containing, bearing is what brings about a transformation so fundamental that a shift away from I takes place; though it is a slow process of gestation, it is irreversible. It is of real importance to know that I cannot make or control this change, I being my own obstacle. My role in this happening is that of a willing sufferer or victim. It is painful because of willingly making house-room for those parts I have striven all my life to exclude, and it is frightening because I am not in control but have delivered myself to what I do not know and cannot know, to something I can only begin to understand by having practiced already. From this practice arises of itself, by hindsight, awareness of what actually is at stake. This calls for great, almost passionate sustained courage, and – in the absence of faith – for implicit trust in the reasonableness of this process of growth. It demands utmost integrity and honesty, refuses to put up smokescreens against what seems totally unacceptable, and will not unheedingly pass over the least unpleasant feature. It is a real labour of love, because we can be sure that on this way we are not spared acquaintance with any inadequacy or weakness inherent in us, and unless we willingly suffer its presence without giving it outward expression, the re-collecting, containing and transformation cannot take place. Growing whole is also growing round, and we are all of us more or less lop-sided. Once more, this containing cannot be done by I, in the mind, but is physical, done in the body which is the seat of our emotional energy that rises, wild and irrational, whenever something pricks me in a weak spot, or threatens *my* dear image or considered opinion.

It is interesting to notice that in their developmental treatment neither the Jungian way nor our native religion, Christianity, take much account of the physical body. Reference to it is lacking in our usual religious ideas. So it might be helpful to have a look at why such an attitude could have come about. It may suggest things which can be followed up, pondered, amplified – or merely left aside.

Chapter Seven

The Cross and the Circle

DAY AND NIGHT follow each other and comprise what we are pleased to call a day, though we still refer to a period of fourteen such days as a fortnight, and the term sennight (seven days) became obsolete not all that long ago. Now we light up the night to avoid darkness; we cling to the light, the sky, the sun. We cannot see what lurks in the darkness at night. Its luminary, the moon, has its own cycle and seems fickle. The star-spangled night sky evokes our sense of wonder and awe. Since we cannot see in the dark, there is little we can do, and so we are delivered to what is within us, to our fears and longings, and our dreams. By day we are distracted by the outside; by night we are 'home' in ourselves.

The waxing and waning moon, closely associated with plants, the sea and fertility of the womb, is poetically 'she' with us, a goddess in pagan times, but was earlier 'he', the fertilizer, consort-god of the Great Mother. From her everything derives, and it is her image we first behold in the human being that gave birth to us.

Her domain is the circle, life everlasting, birth, death and renewal. Every spring sees its flowers and lambs, every autumn its fruit. Life renews itself in profusion; the individual forms, bearers of Life, are dispensable, of little consequence, only seed and fruit. Coming to be, ceasing to be, and returning. Change is cyclic, ever-repeated renewal.

But there is another type of change, which is also inherent in the cyclic change as from seed to flower to fruit, from youth to maturity. This is the domain of 'Father Spirit', not just the fertilizer of the ever-same, but a shape-shifting vector, from amoeba to man, ever evolving, unfolding. The direction is one-way only, of no return. Endless change, too, but in form, not of the form. Growth, yes, but in the sense of development, of new departures; not renewal of the same but irreversible change as such.

Whereas in the realm of the Mother renewal is seen in the same returning, in that of the Father it is seen in Being itself evolving by change. These two forces, vectors, or functions of Life are the first differentiation of the One Life, and most mythologies picture them as a parental pair. Truly, the one cannot be without the other. Between them they have brought about all that is, the manifold differentiations into the 'ten thousand things'. As forces they are not separate, but inhere in every individual form. Differentiated, 'pictured', as a parental pair, they have been at work since the beginning of time, in dialogue, then as now. Portrayed in various ways as suits the beholder, their true features are hidden by the veil of the Divine, totality, wholeness, of which they are two complementary aspects. One of them denied leads to imbalance, stagnation, and unless redressed, to 'ceasing to be'. All individual forms must die, but cultures and species also become extinct.

The Great Mother, her retinue and her mysteries were revered around the Mediterranean in pre-classical times. Specifically in Greece, invading northern warriors brought with them sky-gods, and from their acculturation arose the classical age of Greece and Rome. With a whole family of gods and goddesses emotional perceptions were differentiated – gods and goddesses of love and war, of craftsmanship and art, of growth and fertility, but also of death and mystery; above all were the parental pair of the thunderer and his restraining spouse. But with the bright sky-gods the mystery went underground, and so the gods became all too human and familiar, no longer counterbalanced by dark and depth. A tall tree must grow deep roots. Too bright, even the gods lose meaning. Thus mystery cults began to be imported from Egypt and Asia Minor, vying with each other until one emerged as the established new religion sternly replacing the old pantheon.

Spirit strives on, ever upwards. Earth and ocean hold and retain. The horizontal and vertical vectors in their interaction, the 'dialogue between the sexes' as it were, has been in progress ever since the one, the One Great Mother, the 'Dark Female' as she is called in the Daodejing, the Mysterious One of many names, divided in our perception into the great parental pair with their fatal numinosity who between them beget all that is. They are still acting in all that is. How futile to try and refute or deny one in favour of the other.

In our cultural development which favours the Sky-God, Father Spirit, the Great Mother has been reduced to 'mere matter', with the result that the Father has been all but forgotten, too. Like children distracted by marvellous toys, we played recklessly the most exiting games of progress and supremacy, defying the Mother who would hold us in bounds. And now, wearied, and sobered by our despoiled home, we begin to miss her, for we no longer know what to do. Having also lost the Father in our 'progress', we truly are abandoned orphans.

When the gods, or God (and his adversary, the devil) lose or seem to lose their power, become familiar, 'nothing but', that is paganism, then as now; a being carried away by unbridled emotions, whether these be of the flesh or, more perniciously, of an idealistic fanaticism. The classical paganism of the flesh metaphorically cried for salvation and makes the rapid spread of Christianity understandable, with its denial of the flesh and its exclusive orientation towards the spirit. And that is falling once more into one-sidedness. Where is the spirit now, the numinosity, awe and wonder? How we miss it – for it has become reduced to nothing but mind, I. And the mantle of the numinous does not fit human shoulders! We try to grasp, thus miss the enlivening touch. We have ideas about it, thus fail to respond to it.

Can we go still deeper, closer, to illustrate our perennial attempts to render a force which in itself is invisible, imperceptible, incorporeal, which can only be experienced? And yet is indispensible for our well-being and development both individually and culturally, because it gives sense and meaning? The attributes that have always been felt as belonging to this force are power, warmth and light. This force, unknown and unknowable, yet evokes our response. It works in us and around us, in everything that is, animate or inanimate. Sensing it and responding, just this is what religion means, in depth.

Crystals are classified by an assumed axial system according to which they seem to grow. These axes do not exist in themselves, though crystals do grow accurately in obedience to these non-existent constructs; and so do animate beings, according to their 'nature', to give these constructs another name. And though no two rock crystals, or two apples, or cats, are exactly alike, they are yet unmistakably what they are, and in their limited uniqueness express fully that of which they are a specific and differentiated product. Thus all things form, transform, develop, evolve. The wonder, awe and miracle are in beholding this whirligig of cyclic, changing, evolving unfoldment.

In the apple pip slumbers in potential the apple tree. In an egg, fertilized, develops a chicken; and in another type of egg, fertilized, a human. That spirit should be inherent also in rock crystal and organic sludge seems like blasphemy, but where otherwise would we be, or the sludge? How can matter be inanimate when we ourselves are composed of it? This is easier to take now than fifty years ago.

The horizontal cyclic, and the vertical, evolving vectors interact, have been at work since time began. Time began with them as did everything else. Without them time is not, nor space, nor are they – or we. Most mythologies portray this emergence of the primal pair from the undifferentiated as a split between heaven and earth, when the one static non-corporeal is-ness or being-ness bifurcated into two who then brought forth all that is. Or divided into two poles along which the basic energy can slide, anode and cathode, opposite and complementary. How tremendous that basic energy is we know concretely since we learned to split atoms and experienced an aspect of it! Strong enough to hold the stars in motion, not concerned with our earth alone, it is so vast and distant, so immense that the mind reels, and if open, is touched once more by that sense of awe and wonder which is our birthright. This is the right response to it, by which we are put again into phase, re-aligned once more to that which is and works in us. We are moved to good if we are in phase, obey, respond rightly, swing in accord with it; or moved to bad and pain, shattering, if we swing in discord, disobey this power that made us, which acts in us and of which we, the individual forms, are carriers – as is the atom. Like the atom, if we split too far, can no longer phase in or tune in, if we can no longer contain, then a devastating power is released. The primal pair may be differentiated but must remain in dialogue, must interact. Split into real separation it reverts to the one which in its totality cannot be endured or contained by the individual, thus the resultant destruction.

The awe of God is a very real perception, not to be tampered with. It is only human that we human beings have come to perceive this tremendous power in our shape though it was not always so. It could be in a stone, too, or in a mountain. But 'from the time since the beginning' we have accorded it the attributes of The Divine and revered it under many forms, either as the one, or differentiated as many, but ourselves always subservient to it. The adventure of our day, the unprecedented possibility beckoning, is the enlivening, quickening, healing and aware recognition of this power which is our ground of being, no longer swaddled into any forms or dogmas. And our response to it in reverence and wonder, is a re-linking and rededication in service.

Meanwhile, with the advent of Christianity, which we still have not understood after 2000 years, our culture elected the Father, and of late, in the headlong progress since our scientific enlightenment, has well-nigh forgotten him too if we are not tacitly convinced that we have outrun him. And so, on the brink of disaster and shipwreck, the swing inevitably goes back to the Mother once more, as the Assumption of the Virgin in Catholic dogma exemplifies, or Robert Graves' 'The White Goddess'. Also his 'Black Goddess', for it is an unconscious swing back, accompanied by all the darkness and murkiness that clings to her primitive layers – occultism, drugs, violence, and a desperate longing for some at-one-ment.

On whichever side of the great divide we as individuals stand, it might be useful to reflect where we have actually landed ourselves and now stand, rather than fretting about where we keep on running to. Why are we so keen on aims and purposes? Could it be that we are frightened to stop and look? That all our running, all our 'progress', is a desperate attempt to avoid acquaintance with ourselves, with our own darkness from which we flee since we have taken to the light? Yet the acquaintance with our real selves is the great adventure, for there is so much more to ourselves than I who think I know myself.

The great mythologies and religions have variously portrayed, even caused us to re-enact in symbolic form, this way of re-acquaintance, of re-discovery, of re-collection – but today, they no longer speak to us. We may hear, or read the words, but miss the message. And so, naked and alone as we feel ourselves to be, we seem to be forced to set out on this way of re-collection, each for ourselves, at our own risk. Why are we so afraid of being alone, of being shorn of all our artificial trimmings, frills and flounces, which we are not, for we were born without them and they leave us at death. Why can we rarely endure our own company as we enjoy that of a good friend? And why the fear?

There is no ready-made answer to this question, but there is the possibility of finding out. This means to learn to endure our own company, our own loneliness, our own longing rather than being carried away into our usual escape routes of distraction; it means just to stay put and find out by not refusing what is or what wells up in us. This surely is the first step towards wholeness. As long as we deny something, that detracts from wholeness.

The circle is the time-honoured symbol of wholeness. The cross symbolizes the two seemingly divergent but interdependent forces of continuation and change, of matter and spirit, mother and father. We are crucified on this cross: accepting the suffering, containing it in willing awareness, constitutes the healing of the split. In it the self-centred childish 'I' dies, and from this feared dark night emerges the true son of man, a whole being.

Chapter Eight

The Interplay
of Dark and Light

IN THE PREVIOUS chapter we met the primal pair as spirit/matter or father/mother, the first differentiation of that tremendous force which has always been experienced as Divine. The Far Eastern, specifically the Chinese, conception stresses aspects of this pair which are foreign to our culture, thus presenting new perspectives. Perhaps the most startling but also most helpful is the total neutrality of this pair and their interplay or functioning, a kind of three-in-one power of awesome strength and total wholeness. In this conception there is no split. The total energy does not give rise to a primal pair but is it. Nor is there a split between the pair, rather a self-evolving continuous at-one-ment of the two aspects, each going about its own and the other's business, both bound by and free under the one law, which they are and which has produced all that is, and thus 'in-forms' all forms. Hence decisive for this conception is the complementary nature of this primal pair of forces, constituting a totality, itself moving, changing, coming to be, ceasing to be and evolving, out of its own nature.

The symbol for this is again the circle, in which the two interacting forces are contained in equal strength when motionless, but each containing the seed of the other for balance when it goes into movement, like a see-saw, so that reverse movement can set in and neither can take over. It is thus self-regulating.

A further point is that this pair, as distinct from our accustomed 'light and dark', which denotes the split, is usually referred to as 'dark and light', 'Yin and Yang', not as a preference for the two are equal and opposite, but as our first possible perception of what is primal, ineffable, 'dark', Laozi's 'mysterious female'. In that, the continuity of the whole with part is unriven, and acts all the way in multiplicity, as in the Daodejing, Chapter 25:

> Man obeys the laws of the earth
> Earth obeys the laws of heaven,
> Heaven obeys the laws of Dao
> Dao obeys its own intrinsic nature.

We are here concerned with the primal pair rather than with the Dao as such. What emerges from the above verse is the concept of the accord, harmony and rhythm of everything. If this becomes conscious, 'known', man too is in accord with Dao. It is then not he who acts but Dao acts in and through him; and just this is man's virtue, his strength and power as expressed in the title of the above-mentioned treatise, 'The Way and its Virtue/Power'.

It is therefore not only Dao which, according to context, is understood in a twofold meaning, but De, too, as the energy function sliding between the poles of Yin and Yang, and as the virtue/strength/power that 'informs' the 'man of Dao', the man in accord with Dao.

Virtue (De) is here used in its original meaning of strength, from the Latin meaning of inherent power. It is the strength of restraint, the strength of containment which is fashioned by discipline. It is the moral strength of restraining unbridled appetites or impulse, the strength that contains emotional onslaughts without being carried away. That is what 'morality' or 'virtue' really means, moral strength by virtue of which we remain human! This virtue/power of the Dao acts, 'informs' everything concerned specifically with human activity.

The Neo-Confucian conception of this energy sees it as the inter- acting vital force or life energy. The heart as life-spring is its abode where it is contained in its motionless aspect, and when it goes into motion, it flows through the heart into action. Being naturally in accord with the Dao, it has supra-individual connotations direct with the Dao. Thus, if unobstructed, if the heart is empty (*mushin*), if there is nothing in it, if it is free of self-bias, free of my wishes, loathing, fears, of my ideas of gain and loss, of life and death, then the whole strength of the Dao acts unhindered, 'right' because in accord with what is. My wishes, etc., interfere; they obstruct, constrain and/or warp this 'right' action which then becomes inadequate at best, or blind compulsion which is destructive. Both are 'wrong' because out of harmony, out of phase.

Energy as such cannot be seen, it can only be perceived in the work it does. From that perception the concept of energy is formed. Its source itself is inconceivable. The Dao cannot be seen, cannot even be named, for 'The Dao that can be named is not the eternal Dao.' It can be talked about as 'Way', as energy can; but directly, it can only be responded to, not 'beheld'.

Specific training disciplines help to disentangle and free the heart-energy from the stranglehold of 'I', of my desires, my wanting to possess it, of my itch to manipulate things, my trying to bend the energy to my purposes. In proportion to that, the energy again comes into phase with the Dao so that it can freely flow, act and respond in accord with the situation.

In an animal this happens 'naturally'. We have to relearn it, in the sense that I have to be out of the way for this to happen, the heart 'self-emptied'. Thus the learning is not a matter of how I can do it, nor is it a blanking out and letting the energy erupt elementally, a-humanly, but is a Way along which I, full of wants, subject to bouts of sudden anger, stuffed with opinions, etc., become ever less, ever more empty. Instead there emerges 'a man of the Dao', a true and responsible human being, capable of acting as such always, under all circumstances. This releases the free flow of the vital heart-energy which as a vitalizing and enlivening force makes for health and well-being, as well as for 'right action', the right response to a given situation.

Sumo wrestling as seen in Japan is a marvellous demonstration of these two aspects of energy – motionless and in motion. Two colossi, motionless but fully collected, and then the sudden, coordinated spring into action. The bout is over in seconds; the tremendous momentum this way or that, and then having spent itself, returns to the motionless. However, the form must not be mistaken for the energy though the energy displays itself in the form, and the form's conductivity, its 'in-phase-ness' is a decisive factor. The more interference there is with the free flow of the energy, the more self-will, self-consciousness, or fear, the more the form suffers, inherently and in its performance. Red-hot wire coils are soon burnt out because of their resistance to the flow of electric current.

In the human realm, 'I'-interference, 'I'-bias, 'I'-centredness, throttles and obstructs the free flow, because of 'I'-volitions. This is the real meaning of the enigmatic term *wu wei*, so often mistranslated as 'non-action'. But it is not a state of disengaged inertness, rather a swinging in phase, in and with the Dao, in which joy, the zest, the liveliness, the sense of play truly emerge, whether in rest or in motion. And that is totally different from inertness, not a deadening of our true human faculties but a quickening of them.

In Buddhist terms, this corresponds to liberation from 'I' and thus from 'I'-volitions, that is, all my opinions, firm convictions, views, judgments, etc., even my ideals. It is these, manifesting in thought, word and deed, which are our bane for they bind us, and are the Karma-producing agents. In accord with the Dao, the Buddha-heart energy acting itself, no Karma is created, and so, though there is action, it leaves no trace.

From the side of 'I', this means not to attempt to grasp the energy. Such attempts are futile, for as such it is not there. It can neither be found nor seen, but it can be responded to, totally – which for us human beings also means humanly responded to, not as an animal, demon, hungry ghost or heavenly being. Master Rinzai warned his pupils against attempts at grasping at this energy, 'When you seek it in the moving, it turns motionless, when you look for it in the motionless, it has taken to moving.' And that the form – I, or my body – may not be mistaken for the animating energy, the 'Diamond Sutra', a classic text of Northern Buddhism, puts these words into the mouth of the Buddha:

Who seeks me in form,
Who searches for me in sound,
Misguided are his footsteps.
He cannot find the Tathagata.

Nor is this warning totally unknown in our own culture, or what else is the command against the fashioning of graven images about? But we are enthusiastic makers of pictures, of concepts, which we then mistake for real, as we are prone to mistake the finger pointing to the moon for the moon. Yet nobody has ever swallowed the printed menu in mistake for a three-course dinner!

Though it 'in-forms', is inherent in all forms, this vital energy is neither the same as, nor as such, separate from the form. This is the point we need to keep in mind most carefully. It is difficult to encompass, for our Western intellect is a sorting mechanism that distinguishes between this and that: snow is white, grass is green. But when it really comes down to it, and this is what makes modern physics so hard to grasp, though the apple does indeed fall with a thud, when we go deeper into things, light already seems to behave paradoxically, sometimes moving as waves, and sometimes as particles. Since the split of the atom, modern physics has had to conceive matter as a network of forces. It has been said that it takes five years to acclimatize a student to this new thinking. A good example of how hard it is to remodel our accustomed thinking – even in one discipline only. Small wonder the new thinking in physics is not yet generally accessible. And in a wider connotation, the link between 'as inside, so outside', that is, that we view the world according to how we think, has as yet barely been touched.

Systems of thinking – if they are not futile speculations or the uninformed straddlings of beloved hobby-horses – derive from the impact, the experience of this energy. The full response to it triggers the urge to render it perceptible and to share the immediacy, the spontaneity of the impact/response, but this presupposes that the response was made in awareness, and was in phase with the Dao. As that it is diametrically opposed to the impulsive, puppet-like reaction which surges up in excess to the impact stimulus. But blind or aware, obedient to this energy we are; in that we have no option. 'In phase', it compels right response, right action and thus is a guide, yet its very compulsion misleads the blind like a 'will-o-the-wisp', turning destructive as all imbalance does, so redressing the balance. The self-regulating principle of Yin and Yang in action.

If I grasp a live wire, it will certainly make me dance like a puppet, but I come off much the worse from this encounter. Again, the animal's response to this energy is accurate and so in the animal the energy acts as its guide, informs it in both senses of the word, as it does all manifestation. We have split ourselves from it by our 'I'-bias, and thus have placed ourselves notionally into Samsara and suffer, as the Buddha pointed out when he awakened from this delusory dream. 'The Dao obeys its own intrinsic nature' and everything flows with it. We human beings, aware only of our limited 'I' with our correspondingly limited 'I'-views, have sprung ourselves out of this contained guidance, notionally freed ourselves from it, and now we suffer from this delusory separation. In this precarious position, we yearn for a return home which, to be effective, needs to be a pilgrimage, a labour of love, leading to a self-emptying and thus awakening to the awareness of all things as they really are. A return to paradise, unconsciously being contained without bestirring ourselves at all, is no longer possible after the conscious recognition of separation has arisen. Hence the angel with the flaming sword! So we must strive forward.

This states the problem with which we are concerned in the next chapter: 'The Way Home'. It is not a new way, decked out in fancy dress or exotic garb, but is as old as the world, as familiar as our daily life. Do we really live our daily life or do we more or less go through the motions, our attention mostly elsewhere, avoiding what we do not fancy, bemoaning our bad luck, or playing a role like an actor on a stage? Like puppets, compelled by we know not what? Again, in the words of Master Rinzai:

'Look at the puppets prancing on the stage
And find the one behind who pulls the strings.'

He who pulls the strings is the whole man, re-collected from his fragmentation, re-aligned and wholly human. Out of this state he responds wholly, spontaneously, in full awareness, and thus 'rightly', that is, as appropriate to the situation.

Chapter Nine

The Way Home

EVER SINCE MAN WOKE UP from primordial sameness, or ate from the tree of knowledge of good and evil, or became conscious, he felt himself separate, alienated and alone. To be conscious is to be able to 'see', to reflect, and to differentiate what is seen into this and that – a spoon or an apple. No judgement is applied in this. The original sin seems to have been self-biased judgement which severed the seer from the seen, rather than just seeing which reflects like a mirror what is seen. Ever since this separation, driven out of paradise, man has yearned for and striven towards recapturing wholeness.

The mythic formulations upon which man's religions have been based are pointers or pathways towards wholeness. If lived rather than studied, they reconnect the part with the whole. There is, however, the proviso that in their formulations they must match the level of development of the practitioner. Hence the difficulty of a highly-developed religion like Christianity preached to primitive people with often disastrous consequences; or the impossibility for the dissatisfied Westerner trying to go back or to grow back into a noble savage, or into a state of primordial innocence.

A growing back into sameness, into paradise, is not possible for a man who has lost his innocence, and who, with his highly developed consciousness, sees differentiation but mistakes it for separation. So it is said that man is prevented from returning to this lost paradise by the angel with the flaming sword who guards the gate. It is further suggested that a state of differentiation, a pilgrimage with all the hardships and perils, is necessary so that he may again return home and inherit his father's mansions.

Man, in accord with nature and as part of it, needs to grow forward, to seek for a conscious, aware re-linking with his ground of being in which he, too, has his being. Thus the unceasing search for it, the urge – continued through the millennia – to render it perceptible in myth and image, or conceptually graspable, a name! But when the spiritual values of a culture become obsolete, these pictures lose their meaning and with it their guiding influence, and are finally replaced by a merely egotistical attitude, 'as it suits me' or 'as I think right', however decked in altruistic garb. Man is impelled to strive after these pictures he himself has fashioned as a moth is drawn towards the light. Hence the warning against the fashioning of graven images – for man is all too prone to mistake the image for what it is meant to portray. As this is unknowable, to mistake the pictures for the ground or essence may be as disastrous as is the moth's flight into light.

In our enlightened days we are blissfully unaware of the awesome numinosity of this ground or essence, however we call or name it. To approach it, from of old, traditional ways of transition were evolved so as to shed the selfish 'I' along the way and thus bring the pilgrim safely home, which entails a rediscovery of and a re-linking with godhead. This term, if thought of as 'the god-head' has become popular, usually with the definite article, but is misleading as it tends to refer to the head and thinking and seat of consciousness. It seems a misinterpretation of the German 'Gottheit', meaning godness, divinity, the Divine.

The formulated gods and deities of all cultures are names and pictures for aspects that point to the Divine, symbols which can and do evoke the sense of the Divine when the religious values are still intact. From the history of religion we learn that gods also come and go, and change. Their features are not permanent. In their various formulations, they constitute the mantle of the Divine which renders the 'totally other' into some perceptible form. A Mahayana saying puts it beautifully when it states that the Buddha's body is the universe, his bones are the mountains, his eyes the lakes, etc., and that it is rendered manifest always and everywhere in a form that fits the perceiving capacity of the beholder.

Like everything else, gods change in form. The Divine, however, is, and has been revered under many names, in many variations and formulae. In us ordinary humans the proximity to the Divine evokes the awe of god. Thus an apocryphal saying of Jesus, 'Who is near unto me is near unto the fire'. Or as we read in the Bible, whenever the Divine, or even a heavenly messenger approaches an ordinary mortal, the first words inevitably are 'fear not'. Only then may contact be established. The proximity of the Divine cuts a man wide open, liberates him from his alienation. In that shudder, man is taken beyond himself; he experiences, takes part in, the Divine.

But the mystics of all ages have rendered this religious experience in a different way. Because man identifies with 'I only', he so to speak lives in shoes too small for him. When a shoe pinches, vision becomes jaundiced, warped. Thus the way of the mystic or sage is a hard one in all traditions, must indeed be so, because it attempts the seemingly impossible, that is, to dislodge the deep-seated sense of 'I'. When this is accomplished, the 'fear not' caution is no longer necessary for only I can fear.

'Purified' from the sense of 'I', after this fundamental shift has occurred, the Divine seems to enter conscious awareness.

In fact, the Divine is inherent in us, as in everything else, as our ground of being. But as long as I am the focus and centre of my consciousness, our separate and limited sense of 'I' has alienated us from this awareness, the perception of, and conscious participation in the life and action of the Divine.

The mystic, as the prodigal son, has returned to this I-less awareness, and henceforth lives it. Since I have an inkling of this but am my own delusion, I like to think of 'states of higher consciousness' with the implicit idea that this is 'my' consciousness, and that I can have these states: so I try to attain them, thus making confusion more confounded.

'I' knows of no other approach, for to I a state of No-I is inconceivable, and moreover, is fraught with fear; hence our fear of death and disintegration. The more so as I have a dim inkling, deep down underneath the 'I'-layer of my consciousness, that on the genuine way towards the Divine there is, must be, the portal of fear and death in which the features of an isolated 'I' are burnt off, and a reforging, a restructuring takes place that ousts I, me, from my top-heavy pinnacle. To I, this is all the more terrifying because the toppling down from that pinnacle forces acquaintance with, acceptance of, and consequently suffering the dark aspect of life which every 'I', whose very nature is selectiveness, fears and shuns because it aspires to light only. Thus the approach to the dark evokes panic, terror.

Yet light and dark belong together, are the two faces of the Divine, as day and night complete each other in a day. There must be death for Life to continue.

The mystic, the sage, divested of I and hence rendered fearless, has entered through this portal of fear and death, has been restructured, reborn. Thus arising, for him – now I-less – it has never existed.

To us ordinary humans, to I, this portal seems closed. Trying to prise it open with impious hands in heedless, childish 'but I want to see, want to know' has dire consequences, as all traditions warn – for to I, on this side of the portal of No-thing, the portal represents the horror of the yawning void. Only when I am purified, have ceased to be I, is the gate found open. It has always been open, non-existent, for it opens unto All which is the 'other' side from that which I know.

This is At-one-ment; it is perceived as Grace, and lived – it is total participation in the wholeness and holiness of all that is. This is the warmth, the goodness, the godliness of the full human state which, bar a few exceptions, we have as yet not even approximated. We are unaware of our inherent plenitude; in the words of Zen Master Hakuin, we are 'in the midst of water yet cry pitifully from thirst.'

We usually mistake awareness for consciousness and vice-versa, because we are dazzled by the common denominator, 'I', who is aware, conscious. But take away the 'I', as in the negative: unconscious and unaware are not exactly the same, are they? I may be fascinated by the book I am reading but unaware that you have for the third time asked me the same question.

Nobody can deny that animals have a consciousness but what distinguishes man seems to be his reflecting consciousness. This faculty is in itself a supreme tool and makes it possible to clearly differentiate what is seen: cats and dogs, spoons, kings, cabbages. So far so good. But since all that I see is regarded as outside, as other than I, the emphasis is on I and thus becomes 'I'-biased. Consequently this reflecting consciousness becomes lop-sided and sees everything my way, as it affects me and my views. This weighing, judging and comparing, and planning ahead, is so deeply ingrained in us that we take it as the most natural thing – my activities! Thus consciousness with us is no longer pure reflection but self-conscious – 'I think therefore I am'; and loaded towards I, the thinker, the head, can become overweeningly and embarrassingly self-conscious in consequence.

So, instead of seeing differentiation without separation, as a garden with manifold flowers, shrubs and trees all harmoniously blending together, comparison splits what is into this and that, into I and you, and taking sides, selects. In the Zen phrase, it 'picks and chooses' and by that has lost its reflecting quality, the 'clear seeing', and so has come under the sway of the 'Fires', their irrationality and compulsion. 'There are none so blind as those who do not wish to see.' This is a very acute proverb. Try to tell an infatuated person, that the object of his idolatry has feet of clay; either the suggestion is hotly rejected and defended, or listened to in blank incomprehension with sullen resentment building up.

Judging that 'I am this' separates me from all that is not-I, outside and inside! The consequence is that I find life and the world not to my liking and for my life to become fuller and more satisfactory, I feel compelled to incorporate all that is not-I (whether worldly or inner riches); and so want arises. 'I want that' – whatever 'that' might be which for the moment has caught my fancy. Thus the want, often enough for a trifling thing, is endowed with the urgency of supreme importance which clearly shows that a lesser, mere trifle, is mistaken for a greater value. It also explains why, if I have successfully possessed myself of what I so hotly wanted, the attraction soon wanes. For basically, what I want, yearn for, is wholeness, breaking out of the delusion of being a separate 'I' and being re-linked again with what is; not apart, but part of.

Not only want, but fear and alienation arise concomitant with this split into I and other. The delusion of I is that though I perceive the yearning, I yearn for knowledge to encompass and for power to incorporate the 'other than I' and thus to feel secure and confirmed. Thus stated, the delusion is obvious, because simply unobtainable. What the delusion masks is the real object of this yearning, wholeness and with it a sense of partaking in what is. As this yearning is inherent in the human heart, it is not and cannot be the province of thinking, and thus cannot be solved by the intellect nor slaked by intellectual knowledge. Thinking and analysing only widens the split, resulting in dry rigidity because the warmth of feeling is lacking. All analysing is bound to miss the essential, or whole, because it singles out. The latter is the province of science which we, split and frightened human beings grab at and misuse to interfere and destroy with. There is nothing wrong with the great achievements of science, but very much with us, the users of it, short-sighted, covetous, aggressive and destructive as we are in this unwholesome state of alienation. The religious ways are tramlines to lead us out of this bifurcation, back into wholeness. Analysing kills the living spirit, kills life – dissects a flower! We learn all about a flower that way, except what makes it grow and blossom. Thus we miss the miracle that quickens. Instead we have many words.

Words serve their purpose, but cannot describe everything. This applies particularly to the field of religious experience.

A church service can be described in detail – the rite, the response of the congregation; folded hands, standing up, kneeling down. What cannot be described is what happens in the heart of the sincere believer as he kneels in the Presence and partakes of the living body. Yet the blessing, the healing, the whole-making, is in that.

This is not meant as a diatribe against thinking which truly is our most precious tool. But if misapplied it is as futile as trying to catch fish with a hammer. So for the purpose of fishing, we leave the hammer that has served us so well and will continue to serve us – but not for fishing.

Fundamentally, I yearn and need to become whole, as a part is subsumed, as an individual wave merges into the ocean. Faith, true faith of the sort that can move mountains, and even more than mountains can also move me, is not in something outside, but is obedience to this yearning that works in me, yet is not me. This is an act of surrender so total as to be inconceivable to I, as inconceivable as that which is 'totally other'. Just this constitutes the other side of wholeness or totality, what is other than I know and can imagine, so totally other from anything I can conceive of that the only approach towards it is in awe, in fear and trembling.

No rational, educated Western 'I' likes to hear such things; it smacks of superstition, the primitive – of all those things our scientific enlightenment has released us from. Has it? Or have we not seen a return of interest, of fascination in all that is irrational, 'occult', from psychedelic drugs to satanic cults and everything conceivable in between – but not the inconceivable.

Yet in all these movements, however bizarre, there is a very genuine groping and effort. The tragedy seems to be that in all these new occultisms or attempts to revive old ones, the long-neglected yearning has become so compulsive that it rises as an irresistible flood and robs I, the son of man, of his birthright, his conscious and informed thinking without which wholeness is equally impossible. The mistake, the blindness of it is that the human faculty, thinking, is sacrificed rather than I. Hence the revolt against authority as overcompensation, or the attempt to grasp intellectually which is grossly limiting and thus failing wholeness. For wholeness is total; attempts at limiting it to the known only, or to the not known, both miss the point. More over, the one who limits, who chooses and takes sides, just that one is in the way. I am my own obstacle and limiting factor, and must remain it. So what is required is not only one of my faculties, however supremely human, not just a medley of ideas or fond fancies, but the whole of me, the surrender of I which also needs to be total – not of the intellect for which I so easily mistake myself.

This naturally frightens me, as the nearness of the Divine evokes awe because it is so inconceivably more, greater, Total. Hence the ways of long training, ways of approach which are safe and total. If mistakenly I do not wish to surrender, but I want to become whole, logically this would mean – though I never think this – that then I would have to incorporate all that is. Of course this is absurd. It would burst me, result in destruction and madness. There are the perennial warnings against such misguided attempts, as against the lifting of the veil by impious hands, for the 'totally other' is destructive to I.

Fred Hoyle's well-known novel, *The Black Cloud*, treats of the same theme, and makes excellent contemporary reading. An Eastern formulation puts it concretely as, 'Do not tell the frog in the well of the vastness of the wide ocean.' The frog, offended, begins to blow himself up with all his might. The outcome is inevitable. Yet stubborn as I am, I still behave as if I could. The stronger the sense of 'I', the more exclusive I am of any other, the stronger I am held in thrall by wanting, aggression, and delusion; if no longer in their crude forms, then their subtle manifestations hold sway, as ingrained views and opinions, or as strange pictures in the mind – my mind, which is another way of saying I. In Buddhism, these three manifestations of primal energy are called the Three Fires, causing conflagration when unbridled and untamed, but when collected and contained are the inexhaustible source of warmth, strength and light.

The last thing that I, any I, wants is to give in, yet this seems to be the necessity in order to reintegrate the alienated part, I, with the inherent wholeness which is not mine. And this reintegration needs to take place in full awareness.

In our time, the loss of our spiritual inheritance has placed us in a precarious position, for quite unconsciously I, every I, has more or less appropriated for myself the mantle of almightiness which is the strength or power aspect of the triune energy. But the mantle of almightiness does not fit human shoulders – no aspect of the Divine can be appropriated by I. Our attempts to do so, however, unaware, bring up the dark side which we try to exclude. Whatever I resist gains power over me. Hence the profundity of such expressions as 'resist not evil'. The inevitable 'I'-reaction to such suggestions is one of fear: 'But if I do not resist it, it will carry me away, and I will do it'; and coupled with that fear is my very real fear of losing control. But this is one of the many delusions from which I suffer. For what I do not resist does not and cannot gain power over me, thus cannot carry me away. What is more, if I do not defend myself against it, then I have to suffer it to draw near, suffer its presence in me which is a true passion. In this passion, this suffering the darkness inside, I am crucified and die. But just by my suffering and death the darkness itself is transformed, liberated. Again, this is the shift from I to No-I on which Buddhism justly lays stress.

When approached by fierce demons, the Buddha, his Presence, his Buddhahood, caused their transformation. And though they always remained somewhat fierce according to their nature, they found their place as the guardians of the Buddha's Law and, partaking in it, living it, remained within it.

Giving oneself into what is, and partaking in it is the way. Not trying to manipulate or conquer and control which is mostly prompted by my fear of otherwise being carried away. The truly heroic act of totally giving in, not blindly but in full awareness, this is what leads into wholeness. And needed for this is first and foremost the virtue or strength to do so with open eyes, so that perception may be possible. In the act of really giving myself over unconditionally, in a total surrender, I am no longer the actor, and I as I know myself am not even the experiencer. As long as I am still there, I am only a non-resisting sufferer. Wholeness I cannot experience, it arises only when I am no longer there. This does not mean loss of awareness, but it does imply a shift, a real re-structuring. It is I who am blind, for I am identified with my mind and that excludes other perceptions.

Drink a glass of water, wholly. The whole entity takes it in, and responds, 'Ah!' Try! Afterwards we can revert to our usual ways, describe it as far as words can go. But that immediate and total response, wholly giving in to the drinking, wholly taking it in, wholly responding, that is the secret.

The virtue or strength is to open up, aware and willing; to allow things, feelings, emotions to touch us, to cut us wide open even if it hurts; allowing ourselves to be deeply moved. If awareness is lost in this, we are carried away into a seizure. But being deeply moved is a whole, total response in awareness and forges a new awareness in the sense of partaking which is the opposite of seizure.

In this being deeply moved and partaking, I as I know myself am dislodged, am re-integrated, and from this state actions are also responses of wholeness, are *wu wei*, total response to the situation as it really is, which is now also perceived in its wholeness. This is the 'clear seeing' of which Zen speaks. But with this is also restored the sense of the miracle and mystery in life, and the fullness, fulfilment, of partaking in it with a loving heart, in conscious awareness, with gratitude. Hence a sense of service, joyfully given. 'How wonderful, how miraculous – I carry wood and fetch water.'

To partake, deeply moved, in the living mystery, and to live this mystery, is what the heart yearns for; it is the fulfilment of the heart, and constitutes wholeness for which there is no measure, which craves no recognition and is its own reward.

In the landscape of spring
there is neither better nor worse;
the flowering branches grow naturally long or short.

Chapter Ten

Going Beyond

The neutrality of the Eastern religious systems is so complete, so total, that the Western mind easily misconstrues them as merely negative, thus demonstrating our bias towards the positive, progressive, hence aggressive. We are orientated to an aim and end, unwilling to stop in the heat of the chase and to take stock. Hence liable to overshoot and go astray, for such an attitude is too one-sided and bound to run itself to a standstill, as all one-sidedness must.

But how is the balance to be redressed, the one-sidedness balanced again, so that going beyond becomes possible, going beyond one-sidedness? A very short scripture of Northern Buddhism may serve as a guide. Its full title is 'The Sutra of the Heart of the Great Wisdom Gone Beyond'. It is, as the title says, considered to be or contain the heart, gist, or essence of all Buddhism. The text exists in both Sanskrit and Chinese. In the latter it is chanted daily in temples and monasteries in the Far East. The following version from the Chinese acknowledges the translations of D T Suzuki in *A Manual of Zen Buddhism* and Trevor Leggett in *The Tiger's Cave*.

The text of the 'Heart Sutra':

The Sutra of the Heart of the Great Wisdom Gone Beyond

By his practice in the Great Wisdom Gone Beyond, the Bodhisattva Kanjizai saw the Five Aggregates to be empty and passed beyond suffering.

Shariputra, form differs not from emptiness, emptiness differs not from form. Form is emptiness, emptiness is form. The same with feelings, perceptions, volitions, and consciousness. All these, Shariputra, are of the nature of emptiness, neither coming to be nor ceasing to be, neither tainted nor pure, neither waxing nor waning.

Thus in emptiness there is no form, no feeling, no perception, no volition, no consciousness. No eye, ear, nose, tongue, body, mind; no form, sound, smell, taste, touch, mind-object; no element of sight, nor any of the others including that of consciousness. No ignorance and no extinction of ignorance, nor any of the others, including old age and death. No suffering, no beginning, no end, no Way. No wisdom, no gain.

Shariputra, by virtue of the Great Wisdom Gone Beyond, and because he gains nothing (from it), the Bodhisattva's heart is not ensnared by obstacles. And where there are no obstacles, there can be no fear. Having left behind all upsetting fancies and dream thoughts, at last he enters Nirvana. All the Buddhas of the Three Worlds have practised the Great Wisdom Gone Beyond and by this means have entered ultimate, peerless, supreme enlightenment.

Acquaint yourself with the Great Wisdom Gone Beyond, the great spiritual mantra, the peerless mantra, the utmost mantra that takes away all suffering, in truth unfailing. Thus the mantra of the Great Wisdom Gone Beyond is proclaimed, is proclaimed as, 'Gone, Gone Beyond, Gone Altogether Beyond, Awakening Fulfilled'.

So, 'by his practice in the Great Wisdom Gone Beyond, the Bodhisattva Kanjizai saw the Five Aggregates to be empty and passed beyond suffering.' The Great Wisdom Gone Beyond. Beyond what? It has often been translated as 'gone to the other shore'; the 'other shore' is a well-known Buddhist analogy, culled from the Parable of the Raft in which the Buddha suggests that though a raft is essential to carry the pilgrim to the other shore, only a dolt would then continue on his way over dry land with the raft strapped to his back. The Buddha likens his teaching to such a raft. The simplicity of such parables is deceptive.

The Buddha summed up his teachings as 'Suffering I teach, and the Way out of Suffering.' The river, in the analogy of the raft, is the river of suffering which needs to be crossed – not avoided. Hence the Middle Way is not just an avoidance of extremes but leads right through the middle of, and thus to the cause and core of suffering, and beyond – to the other shore. Here, on this side, I can have no conception of that other shore. Naively I take it rather like crossing an ordinary river, and expect to continue the way thereafter, now liberated from all suffering. But the river of suffering is no ordinary river. If I believe that the Buddha suggests that I arrive on the other shore, now free to fling away the raft that ferried me over, then I am truly the dolt he warns us not to be. Truly, the river of suffering may be crossed by means of his teaching, but since the sufferer is I, this sufferer remains in the stream, floats away with it. No-I arrives on the yonder shore, the shore of No-thing. Of that shore, nothing can be said – not even the Buddha attempted a description, only asserted that 'even Buddhas do but point the Way.' However, we know that those who crossed that river have not vanished. Like the Buddha himself, they 'came back', embodying the teaching to point the Way. They have become the raft that safely ferries across. This is fundamental to the Bodhisattva ideal.

Nor are this side and the other shore two distinct places in space, they are one and the same. The change is a different attitude, a true change of heart. And so the other shore denotes a state beyond suffering, the state of No-I, of deliverance, Nirvana which, being a state rather than a place, has no abode. And, being a state, it is not just an 'experience'; this should be clear from the consideration that only I can experience something; for No-I, there is No-thing.

Samsara, this side, is what I know or think I know and experience. The Great Wisdom Gone Beyond, beyond I, beyond suffering, bridges those two shores which in the spirit of our text are not separate, not two.

The Maha Prajnaparamita literature, Sanskrit for the Great Wisdom Gone Beyond, is enormous, existing in versions of various lengths. Much of its formulation it owes to that great Buddhist, Nagarjuna. Excellent English translations of this body of literature from Sanskrit originals are available. These texts, needless to say, are guidelines, or astringent medicine to dissolve fancies of the mind or blind belief in words – indeed in anything. They are for deep study, pondering, contemplating, practising, and cutting away the very ground from under the feet of the practiser, leading him beyond the limitations of his 'I', his imprisonment in it. Nagarjuna's great, total, immutable NO slashes off I and returns to No-thing, its ground of being from which it became alienated. Truly, this great NO is 'the sword that kills and gives life'.

The idea of the Bodhisattva is already implicit in the Parable of the raft, is elaborated on in the 'Jataka Tales', but was further developed and deepened by the Northern schools of Buddhism.

The Bodhisattva Kanjizai is better known as the Bodhisattva Avalokitesvara, or in the Far East as the Bodhisattva Kanzeon or Kannon where he also took on female features. A Bodhisattva is one who after practising various stages of perfection arrives at complete I-lessness. 'Where there are no obstacles, there can be no fear'. Where there is no fear, the true warmth of the heart is liberated and can flow unhindered, of its own nature, as the sun shines and needs no objects to shine upon.

Of this particular Bodhisattva it is said that he came to his awakening by the perception of sound, through the sense perception of the ear. Indeed Kannon means 'seeing sound'. Being a Bodhisattva, and moreover one in whom this great compassionate love is particularly manifested, his degree of wisdom, his seeing clearly, is also stressed. The name Kanjizai means to see all things as they really are.

Thus in this first sentence of the Heart Sutra we already have, in a nutshell, the kernel of the Buddhist Way, the liberation of the heart and its inherent warmth which begins to flow of itself when the bonds of I have fallen away by virtue of the practice of seeing but the Five Aggregates – void of an 'I'. With I having become No-thing, voided of all me, mine, there is spacious emptiness. No-thing is thus also the ceasing of 'I'-interference, and this is helped by the realization that the I that I think myself to be is factually only a bundle of Five Aggregates within which no traces of I can be found, a reaction mechanism that comes into operation by outside stimulus but needs no operator. In itself it is empty.

The Five Aggregates or Five Skandhas which make up a human being are thus like the constituent parts which make up a chariot, and dismantled into these, no chariot as such exists. This is one of the main analogies in Buddhism for the non-existence of an independent 'I' as such.

The Five Aggregates are: 1) Form, i.e. the body; 2) Feeling, sensation, reception (of impact); 3) Perception or discernment (of what that impact is – painful, pleasant, etc.); 4) Volition, or volitional configurations and activities (mental) which, because of the I-bias in them, are considered the Karma-producing agents; and 5) Consciousness, the mental faculty of cognition. Whereas 1) is physical, 2), 3), and 4) are associated with mental functioning (the Chinese compound gives 'place of heart', i.e. functioning of the heart/mind), and 5) with the nature of the heart/mind (the Chinese characters give 'Lord of Heart', Sanskrit: *manas*, for this nature, which in the Yogacara teachings is the seventh consciousness and there considered the deluding agent because it mistakes the impressions of the first 6 consciousnesses as 'me', 'mine', and 'I'.)

The Five Aggregates are the chain reaction of our habitual behaviour, but the point is that in the Buddhist formulation the constituent parts of the chariot, or these Five Aggregates are themselves also empty, void of a self-nature and thus impermanent. Subject to change, therefore, they are in continuous flux, causal consequences obeying the law of things as they are, needing no activator or operator for their functioning. In their nature, they are empty.

Buddhism equates I and suffering, seeing I as delusion. Deceiving, hindering, distorting like a mirage, this my deluded vision leads me into one mishap after the other. My views, my clinging to this or that, my wishes or judgement of how it should be, put me into opposition to what is, to things as they really are, and so lead me into disappointment and separation. Though the eyes more or less perceive one's surroundings, the picture-image constructed of this perception may be at variance with what actually has been seen. The usual analogy is like mistaking a bit of rope on the road for a snake. Pure perception would act like a mirror reflecting what falls onto it. In delusion, that mirror is not clear, is painted over with all kinds of squiggles and scrawled sketches, and thus cannot reflect what falls onto its surface; consciousness then can only take note of these false, distorted images.

The next paragraph in the Sutra then really goes into the emptiness of all the Aggregates. Shariputra is the favourite disciple, and the Bodhisattva addresses him, teaching and encouraging him to set his feet in the right direction. In the clarity of his insight and in setting others on the Way to it, therein lies the action of the Bodhisattva. He reveals himself in and as this action.

The tremendous statement of 'form is emptiness, emptiness is form', does, of course, also apply to each of the other four Aggregates. But in this first, bold formulation, it seems to negate all concrete reality. Does it? A thing – in order to be some-thing – needs to have some specific properties to distinguish it from what it is not; it must be either this or that. It cannot be both.

This well-established way of logical, analytical thinking as developed by the Western mind is now sorely tried by the findings of modern subatomic physics. Even light is audacious enough to sometimes behave as waves, and sometimes as particles.

'Form is emptiness, emptiness is form'. Baffled, we try to link this statement to another which, however, denotes something quite different, namely our fabricated dream pictures to which we cling and have painted onto the mirror, which is our heart. Taking the above statement as verbally true, like lotus-eaters we deny reality, grow zombie-like, incapable of living and partaking. This is the heresy of nihilism. On the other hand, to take any thing as unchanging, enduring, is the heresy of eternalism. Buddhism is the Middle Way. This is Nagarjuna's great sword, that once more blazed the trail when that ancient path the Buddha had rediscovered became again overgrown by the brambles of theorizing, by the thickets of wild fancies and speculation. Thus Nagarjuna's fourfold formulation, remorselessly logical, consigns everything to what by nature it is – devoid of self-nature, hence empty. Something, anything, including existence itself, is impermanent, hence compounded or vice versa, and so in itself

Neither:	is;	being;	yes
Nor:	is not;	not-being;	no
	both is and	both being and	
Neither:	is not;	not-being;	yes and no
Nor:	neither is	neither being nor	
	nor not is;	not-being;	neither yes
			nor no

Can we see in this the echo of the Buddha's last admonition to his disciples, 'Impermanent are all compounded things, strive on heedfully'.

'Form is emptiness, emptiness is form'. How far can we follow? Are they simultaneously both form and empty? Does emptiness pervade form like the bouquet pervades the body of a good wine? Or as in the Daodejing, a house is rendered habitable because of its empty space? Or is form a potential of emptiness? Thus far, straining hard on unfamiliar ground, we can venture. Then the sword flashes. No, No, No.

Logical in its formulation, yet concretely inconceivable to *me*, this Great No of Nagarjuna cuts me off, and so is the perilous bridge to the yonder shore. Where there is No-I, there is space, emptiness. This is Nagarjuna's great insight, that Anatta, No-I, is not just the absence of I, all other things remaining equal, but that No-I is No-thing, Anatta is Sunyata, emptiness. With that the mirror is clean. Will remain clean; for with I exists the delusory factor, the fabricator of the pictures, of arbitrary mental constructs. I am truly my own obstacle. When the obstacle has vanished, returned to nothing, there can be no fear. In this spacious emptiness, after the Great No, comes the Great Yes. All things are as they are. Form is emptiness, emptiness is form. Samsara, the world of blind, recurring suffering, is Nirvana; Nirvana is Samsara. No more magic lantern shows, no more deceptive squiggles obscuring the mirror's shining emptiness which now clearly reflects whatever falls onto it, and lets it pass like a cloud without let or hindrance. Thus the mirror of the heart, of reflecting consciousness, remains bright, clear and empty – so sees all things as they really are.

In this clear, reflecting seeing, the teeming world that I knew because I fashioned it from my wants and fears and predilections, has been emptied, has become totally empty, void because No-I. This the next paragraph stresses, carefully leading through the Twelve Links of the Chain of Dependent Origination, which starts with ignorance or delusion; the Chinese ideograms give this Buddhist term as 'obscured clarity' and thus point at that beclouded mirror. From this primal delusion the other links logically follow, each depending on the preceding one; and thus passing through old age and death – as 'ceasing to be' is personally conceived – and finally swinging back as in a circle to its opposite, 'coming to be', that is birth. A continuous re-circling, from moment to moment, from birth to death – the wheel of Samsara. The Twelve Links are: 1) Ignorance or Delusion on which depend 2) the resulting and thus equally deluded Volitions, the fourth Aggregate, from which arise 3) Consciousness, the fifth Aggregate, from which arise 4) Name and Form as form, the first Aggregate, 5) The Six Sense Organs with their functioning – the usual five sense organs with mind/thought as the sixth, from whence 6) Touch/Contact and 7) Feeling, the second Aggregate, giving rise to 8) Thirst/Craving and 9) Clinging/Attachment for 10) Existing/Being with the consequence of 11) Birth and its corollary, 12) Old Age and Death.

From life to life, bobbing up from and sinking back into the 'sea of birth and death', yet also from moment to moment – deluded we all are. Up to the 6th link it is obvious, then 7) pleasant, 8) more, 9) must, 10) have, 11) get, and 12) lose it again.

In their formulation the Twelve Links are an elaboration of the Five Aggregates – and Nargarjuna's Great No cuts through them all. All depend on I; No-I equals No-thing, equals Sunyata, Emptiness. This is the turning of Samsara into Nirvana, the end of suffering.

In Samsara, on this shore, are all the familiar faces, concepts, likes, dislikes, hopes and fears, name and fame, gain and loss – all the ten thousand things, that are and make our world. Beyond that familiar landscape, my speculations can combine familiar parts into strange shapes as I fancy it. The really Beyond, non-spatial, therefore spacious, where there is no-thing, I cannot conceive. How and what could I imagine in the absence of I? How could I, whose very nature is something, imagine no-thing? It is truly beyond I, another world, wide and free – and fearless.

'Only silence, and a finger pointing the Way'. A Way that has been trodden, beckoning on the traveller who has but little luggage left, 'whose eyes are but little covered with dust'. A Way which Buddhas and Bodhisattvas, who themselves have become this Way, proclaim:

'Gone, Gone, Gone Beyond, Gone Altogether Beyond,
Awakening, Fulfilled.'

Chapter Eleven

The Need for Transformation

HERE IN THIS FAMILIAR yet changing world of ours, alienation is important for the process of growing up, and for growing on. Growing up and growing on are the two aspects of the same process, the interaction of that one but bipolar power, force, or energy that is and pervades everything, a living, changing, growing process of becoming – 'the same, yet not the same'. Life is alive, pulsating, growing, dynamic.

Of this one force or power we have singled out two components: a cyclic one of being and a vectorial one of becoming. Their interaction unfolds in an integral pattern, interweaving, one being the other, but when perceived, seeming to be either more this or that. Change occurs in both. That of growing up, from small beginnings to maturity as manifested in the individual form, whether plant or human; and from this comes the intimation that maturity is wholeness, as in a mature tree. Only in us humans does physical maturity not necessarily spell inner maturity. We are separated from that paradise, have lost our innocence; we have even outgrown the days of the revered council of elders, and have become wayward and complicated and very much alone – a precarious position. Physically, we have no options; the child grows up to maturity where the form is 'fixed' – 'the same', continuation as it is.

The other aspect is growing on into what is not the same, a dynamic vector that makes for further development from the norm. And so what from the one side is seen as a fault and weakness, that very cleavage, from the other side is seen as the place of new emergence. It is a potential of what may become, an unfoldment that reaches and affects the whole through the individual where all true change must begin.

And so, growing on, though it starts with the individual, concerns the whole, and is the growing of the whole. But since this is possible through a weakness only, a weakness in the *status quo*, there have been, are, and will continue to be failures. In the neutral but concerted interaction, however, these tend to eliminate themselves when they have become so extreme that they are no longer viable: the swing of Yin and Yang is one of the Eastern formulations. Such total neutrality is foreign to the naive mentality as well as to our purposeful and aggressive (could one say too alienated?) Western mind. We tend to conceive a planner or controller of this process, and attribute the power in all its tremendous, inconceivable totality to the image we have fashioned of it. Since this image has also been fashioned in our likeness, or took on our features because we could not conceive 'more', we have been saddled with the insoluble riddle of why a power to which we attribute only good can also be destructive. The East, though it has been prolific in fashioning images of the most detailed aspects of this total neutrality, has religiously left it alone as inconceivable, and concerned itself with finding a way out from the unpleasant aspects of it.

But to return to the point, a declutching from the *status quo* is necessary for the process of truly growing whole, of growing up and on. Though this seems like a revolt, it is not – and to be clear about it is of real importance today. A revolt refutes, denies, destroys what was – and so only swerves to the opposite extreme. A voluntary declutching is not a denial of what is, but a stopping, a looking round and taking stock and keeping open to the point of being vulnerable. It is from this place of weakness that the truly new arises, nurtured by what was. Wholeness allows no exclusion!

With this, we are now firmly in the province of religion – re-ligio, linking back. How does this look in a neutral setting? A Zen saying states that to begin with, as we ordinarily perceive things, we see trees, and water, and take them unquestionably for just that. Do we ever question our ingrained, culturally fashioned, quite unconscious basic assumptions? The sun goes round doesn't it? We perceive it as that – we do not conceive our world as hurtling round it, spinning round its axis in the process. We may know it in the head, have known it for centuries – but we still cling to our dear illusion, to what is familiar. To know 'home' we must first leave it. It is a wrench that hurts and opens our most vulnerable spot.

So, the Zen saying continues, there must come a second stage, where trees are no longer seen as trees, nor water simply as water. A real process of alienation, where what is known is wiped away, a stage to be suffered through, a softening-up process during which, as in loosened soil, new tender sprouts may shoot.

And in the third stage, trees are after all trees once more, and water is water; they are now really trees just as they are, and water is really water. A Zen priest, when asked whether the third and first stage are not then identical, smiled and answered: 'Well, in a way they are. But in the first stage, for example, look at a baby, it will take things as they are – but then something frightens it and it yells "Mummy!" In the third stage, there is no more need for this yell.'

Approaching somewhat nearer, how does this look? Driven from the warmth and irresponsibility of paradise where all was the same and the lion laid down with the lamb, the eyes, however unwilling, are forced open by necessity, and in the light of day see differences. The lion does not lie down with the lamb; and so acquaintance is forged also with the dark side which every selective 'I' shuns – and thus misses the whole. 'Dark' is not necessarily 'bad'; only I think it to be.

Liberation, deliverance, of which the Eastern systems speak, is not a gain for I but a deliverance from I. The connotations of this widen out beyond the individual. I shun darkness in me: but whatever I refuse gains power over me. Thus deliverance from I is also the liberation of the dark side.

What is light only, easily dazzles, blinds, or deceives like a mirage. What is dark is a potential of warmth and strength; but first we come into contact with its primal, primitive aspect, as blind red rage, violence, lust, or in subtler forms as blind stubbornness invading our ideas, wants, convictions and ideals. Rightly we shun its primal aspect that works havoc in the human realm. But perhaps the right way is to endure and to suffer it, steadfastly holding on to what is human, not being carried away into the primordial Fires which flare in every strong emotion. Moreover, we are pleased to think that the energy in our opinions and convictions is 'mine' and so we are doubly deceived. In their primal aspect, the Fires also constitute for I the terror of the great unknown, the totally other; hence the panic fear of losing control.

To approach those Fires is dangerous. It is also terrifying. Only a hero can do it, often assisted by an animal or some helpful spirit. This is a theme that runs like a thread through all cultures and ages. Is bringing back the fire such a tremendous event merely because it is used for heating and cooking? Could that arouse the envy of the greatest gods? Is not fire a god in its own right? Why are offerings burnt in a sacrifice – to be 'sent up' to the gods? Can we find a link here, a magic by analogy, a symbol of immense depth which still holds us spellbound, awed, and so suggests another aspect – the propensity of fire to get out of hand, and so needing to be carefully guarded against breaking into conflagration? And is the hero who brings back a little of this fire perhaps the one who in himself has tamed the primal flame which is inimical to the human realm but which, gentled and carefully tended, is strength/power that energizes, enlivens, and gives warmth and light?

Could this be what makes us truly human: that the fire is itself transformed, thus no longer carrying us away? This is perhaps what the true hero stands for, and the religious traditions know it. Whatever their formulations, their training ways are remarkably similar; by the very nature of the endeavour, they must be hard, dangerous and sometimes terrifying. The lives of the great religious founders, of the great mystics of all ages and climes, are variations of the same theme. Common to all, when it comes to the point, is that there was no resistance – they 'gave in'. Gave in to what? That is the wrong question. They gave in in the sense that they did not turn away. For again, all that is denied, refused, resisted, defended against, that by the act of denial gains power over one and then turns destructive.

This giving in is cultivated on the religious way, and culminates in a very real 'passion', the 'dark night of the soul', a suffering in and out of the dark, which is the opposite of being carried away by the Fires (the energy discharging itself, depleting the carrier) or resisting it (repression).

Could any man, even as advanced as the Buddha was when he sat under the Bo-tree, have withstood the onslaughts of

Mara, lust, aggression, fear, if he had not been divested of all he was, no-thing left? Or Jesus on the cross? Fully open, not resisting anything – the pain, the shame, and the lance? This is the end stage, only no-thing can pass that portal.

The Western mythological hero slays the dragon, and soon afterwards comes to a sticky end on account of his own *hubris*. The Eastern sage somehow must have gentled the dragon which symbolizes the spirit, carrying the golden ball of wholeness. There the dragon is the steed of the sage, flies with him through the air. Air and flying denote the spiritual state in this old picture-language.

Once the discipline of restraint, the daily life practice of giving oneself to the job at hand and staying with it, has settled in somewhat, and the collection of the body and re-collection of the wayward heart has become somewhat familiar, the next step is to work on the transformation of the emotional Fires.

For a true transformation to take place, a hermetic vessel is needed. For us, the human body is that vessel. And the transformation is worked by discipline voluntarily undertaken, a discipline of giving in and of suffering things out in patient awareness, steadfastly, without being stampeded out of the human, of our human qualities. No longer deflected by I, me, mine. Suffering our own emotional reactions, wants, wildness, fears, darkness, in humility and steadfastness, holding to the little, not forsaking our humanity, that is the Way. 'Be humble and you will remain whole', says the 'Daodejing', the treatise of the Way and its virtue/strength. Real strength is needed for enduring, strength that can hold, and continue to hold to the small, the gentle, the meek, when the primal Fires flare. From the side of we ordinary people, this has always been felt to be a superhuman quality. Factually this is what makes us truly human, wholly human, whole; meanwhile we are aware only of our fragmentation. This is why we are so easily carried away. Thus the work, the great opus, is for I to become so steadfast, so small, in fact no-thing, that there is nothing to be carried away any more, nothing to be driven out or tempted out of the human realm, thus no longer capable of being swept away to become god or demon or animal or whatnot.

Our times are violent, full of aggression and fear. Yet few of us have actually seen death – or we have vicariously seen only the lurid forms with which the media regales us. We fear it the more. We do not see peaceful death, the dignity and majesty of death. So we miss its promise. Only I can die. Life continues.

Again we return, once more, to the analogy of the waves and the ocean. If everything else has failed, death restores us to what we are; it is not an end but a beginning. Said a Zen master: 'When that moment comes, there is nothing more you can do; you fold your hands and go with it to where you always have been.' Or, as we read in the Heart Sutra, 'Where there are no obstacles, there can be no fear.'

We are part of a whole which is not static but a vast process of becoming which we, being some of its parts, can help or hinder but, fortunately, can neither make nor undo. But we can experience it. Blind, frantic, heedless, we are the nightmares of this wholeness which needs the faculties it evolved to grow towards becoming aware itself. Thus, wholeness itself needs the eyes of human consciousness, sight purified from the taint of 'I-only', to wake up and to see. In this seeing, wholeness beholds itself; or more neutrally expressed, wholeness has become aware of itself.

Meanwhile we are all too easily exploded by our primitive emotions or by our emotionally charged opinions, wants and aggressions, by our defence-manoeuvres which cover the underlying fears, and so we dance like puppets on the rim of a volcano inside which the primal Fires heave. We have never learned to contain our emotions, only to repress them or to discharge them. We became unbridled, the more so in times when nothing else gave us pause or bulwark. Depending on the cultural swing, we older ones were reared to learn to repress, hence the opinionated rigidity that is the typical result of such uneasy repression. Discharge is the modern answer as its extreme opposite, and is the supposed cure for all. But is it? Release methods may bring temporary relief but as they cure the symptoms rather than the cause (of which these methods are unaware), no real change is wrought, and like a drug they become addictive, and debilitating as less and less energy can be contained. Trends swing between these two extremes – the Middle Way is more demanding, not just a trend.

The discipline of learning to contain, in full awareness, the dark side in which the Fires flare, this is the way towards wholeness. The way implies suffering the presence of the dark side, suffering it without avoidance, without defence, neither giving way nor being carried away, suffering it to draw near, and nearer. That suffering confrontation is death to I, the Great Death of which Master Hakuin speaks. In that 'passion' of suffering a shift occurs, the emotional energy itself undergoes transformation. And with that a re-union has taken place.

This is what all religions point to, however diverse in their symbolism, and what they 'teach' in their training ways, which are so remarkably similar. The human heart is what we all have to share, just as we all share its yearning for wholeness, for the openness and warmth of Life, and for awareness of partaking in this mystery of Life; and this partaking is for the sake of all of us, for the peace of all of us, and for the joy of all of us.

Though it begins at home, from humble origins, it is the mightiest task, because limitless and open-ended, and is the true Buddhist practice which cannot be done for oneself alone; it fans out into the surroundings, affecting everything. Deliverance from I, the hallmark of Buddhism, is also liberation of the dark side. Doctrinally it is therefore said that the whole earth, all its creatures and spirits, rejoice when one individual awakens. We might do well to ponder the awesome depth of this saying: the rejoicing of all there is at but one being awakened to such total seeing – for this lightens the darkness.

How is this done, how instigated? Our emotional reactions are whole, total. But since they are compulsive, hence blind, they are totally in excess of what the situation warrants, making mountains out of molehills. Thus they tend to be hurtful and destructive.

To give house-room to these reactions when they arise, to endure and suffer their presence, while continuing with the job at hand, constitutes the discipline in daily life. What is needed is a conscious act of giving oneself over, an aware suffering. My mistake is to labour for what is not my province. 'I want wholeness', so I strive after it and forget to do, or deem unimportant, what I validly can do, my part, the suffering of the emotional onslaughts, while nevertheless giving myself conscientiously to what I am just doing in my daily life, whatever the job or chores. *My* liking or disliking them is irrelevant. The transforming factor lies in the effort of wholly giving myself, and by so doing grace emerges. It is truly given if I but stick to my part.

With grace is also given the strength, the warmth and the light of a joyous partaking, which is a service by living the wholeness of life, of what is, and living fully because deeply moved by the mystery and miracle of what is.

Chapter Twelve

Maps for the Journey

'EVEN A JOURNEY of four thousand miles starts right under one's feet', states a Chinese proverb. So in our training we are again and again encouraged to 'look at the place where one's feet stand'. It takes a long time to heed this, even longer to appreciate it. We are heedless and hasty, preoccupied with ourselves, our likes and dislikes; we are keen on progress, always chasing something. The far-off or far out beckons because the grass always looks greener in the next field – does it not? And familiarity breeds contempt. We think we know the place where our own feet stand only too well – that is why we want to get away from it! Accordingly we feel almost slighted, set back, when told to just look there, in the seemingly familiar. 'That is not what I have come for.' Do we really know the place where our feet stand, have we ever truly bothered to stop and look? Or do we but think we know it and feel no need to give it a glance? Underneath all these thought-coverings of my assumptions about it, is there perhaps also a persuasive whisper, 'Better not'? Could it be that this is why we are so keen to avoid it, to run somewhere else so as not to find out what there is? For much is to be found at the place where our own feet stand. We ourselves stand on it, physically with our own feet.

Every 'I' feels itself separate from all else that is; but this is delusion, and so deep down there is an inherent yearning to 'get out'. This yearning is true, a prompting to get out of the delusion, to be re-linked again to what is. The dilemma is that I, being deluded thought, mistake this yearning as an irresistible urge to rush away from what I feel to be unsatisfactory and strive towards an imaginary goal of contentment. Thus I, my thought-streams of delusion, are for ever 'on the way', flowing *from* the delusory thought of I *to* an equally delusory end-state which, being illusion, is not obtainable. This is the full measure of what the Buddha called Suffering, one of the hallmarks or signs of human existence.

These endless thought-streams occupy my waking day and are the cause of my inability to remain in the here and now, at the place where my feet stand. Would I but look at it and truly get to know it, it becomes the place of deliverance. We are reminded of the Buddha's 'immovable spot' on which he sat down vowing not to get up until he 'saw'.

Do I really expect that those figments of my mind, coveting imaginary end states, can be concretely realized by me for ever after, happy and content? Or that, picking and choosing as is my nature, I could be content for ever after even in an abode of bliss?

Should my thought-streams, I, conceive the irresistible urge to stand on the sunlit peak of a Himalayan mountain, and should I have the money – and time – to gratify this urge, two courses are open to me. A deluded one which takes no thought but presses for instant results because overlaid by the intensity of 'my' picture with no experience in mountain climbing, nor forethought of what concretely awaits me on that peak, I can hire a powerful helicopter and within a day – instantly! – have myself lowered onto this coveted peak, just as I am. How long would I survive the cold and blast?

> The Himalayas of the mind
> Are not so easily possessed.
> There's more than precipice and storm
> Between you and your Everest.
> H T BAHNSON

If I really want to stand on that peak, concretely with my feet and return to tell the tale, my first step towards it – if otherwise physically fit – is at the sandstone cliffs near Tonbridge Wells! There I can begin to learn the art of mountain climbing. How pedestrian, when I want to soar! Who wants to, and who thinks he can ascend such a peak without adequate preparation?

However deluded my thoughts, to differentiate I from the primal urges, is the first step or stage in the long, arduous journey towards wholeness. For this, training is needed, and a training yard – the place where one's own feet stand – a circumscribed precinct which contains and from which it is impossible to break out. This sounds austere. So, if it is to work, it can only be entered voluntarily. For the beginner, things are not laid on too heavily at first. Since his own attitude, his wishing to do the training, is the important factor, he also must know what the containing fences are for. And it must be his own considered choice that he goes within them to 'work himself out'; the stress is on 'himself', not on 'out'. Thereby hangs the tale – and the practice.

Though it may irk and sometimes feel like a prison, yet what circumscribes also becomes familiar and within the known boundaries there is security. 'In the landscape of spring, there is nothing better or worse; the flowering branches grow naturally long or short.' Life is not hemmed in by any boundaries, and is as whole within as without; for the one who can settle within fixed boundaries, there are no more pressing problems. As the Sixth Patriarch said, 'The peasant lives it every day though he is not aware of it.' Few nowadays can do so, we are too unsettled. And so willy-nilly we are forced to go the religious way, to seek for a meaning. Life, which is also our true nature, compels us to undertake this quest. But the religious way is the way within, not the way further and further out. So we need to heed the place where our feet stand!

This is what we really need to know today. We cannot break out from Life itself. Yet, fenced in we cannot settle; hence the dilemma. We are strung between the urges towards 'out and away' or 'more'; and if neither seems possible, we regress, and either turn savage, or naively and ineffectively pseudo-primitive. All these are merely versions of the same mistaken outside trend.

But we can also 'turn within' while keeping to the place where our feet stand. From that circumscribed place, or training yard, the inward way opens. It leads down into the depths of one's own nature. On that inner way there are many blind alleys and pitfalls. They are well charted. We do well to acquaint ourselves with a good map of this inner landscape if we want to reach its unplumbed depth.

So the first step on this inner way is not into uncharted territory, but right into a fenced-in training yard, the place where our feet stand, our ordinary daily round. At first it irks as too narrow, too circumscribed. Training places are like that, feel tight to me, seem enclosed, contrived, and very different from what I expected – the opposite of what I want. Yet boundaries exist; we cannot always do as we like, have what we want, get rid of what we loathe; there are limits, and within these are joy and grief, laughter and tears. This is the first lesson I need to learn, and it is not learned without bucking and kicking and trying to break out.

Though I am rarely aware of it, what I want above all is to have my will, my way. Yet this so-called will is not mine but is the primal Fire that flares whenever I am denied what I want, feel myself rejected, or find myself out of control in a situation; then the very structure of me seems to be threatened. So the training yard serves both as secure confinement and as stout but resilient fence against which I inwardly can heave and kick, and in the process become less rigid, acquire stamina and strength of endurance, and the art of giving in – for the wall does not give.

We can use our daily life just as it is for that purpose, provided we decide that we will take it just as it is, without shunting it around as it suits me.

Apart from the upbringing that we had as children, in this first stage we voluntarily again undertake a kind of second upbringing to learn self-discipline and acquire staying power capable of sustained effort and endurance. These are all-important prerequisites for the training, and we need to know this to stay the course and to fashion the freedom that makes good use of all circumstances. 'Every day is a good day', says an old master. It entails real effort; mere imitation, outward conformity, is not good enough – and will soon result in lifeless rigidity.

Actually, in this initial stage what is being bounded, circumscribed, is not I – as it seems to me – but the Fires themselves. Unless training is really thorough, unless this stage is really assimilated, it is not conducive to leave the security of the training yard which both exposes and shields, but always contains. Only when the art of giving in rightly has been fully cultivated can and does a great shift occur.

To the considerations of this stage belongs the much maligned concept of morality. It is a loaded term – so we need to look under the surface. What if we take it as 'moral fibre' or 'moral strength' – hence 'inner strength' to endure, even to endure an onslaught of the Fires, of the passions, without being deceived by them, even less being carried away by them? 'By virtue' of this strength we may, for example, remain human instead of being transformed into an angry demon. Moral strength really serves two purposes simultaneously. The obvious one is to keep an individual within the boundaries tolerable to his family and community. Thus in a society with still valid spiritual and cultural values, the moral code is experienced as meaningful, a harmonious expression of these values. The established moral principles are then a support and bulwark for the individual in times of crisis, prevent him from regressing into a primitive state, and keep him human not by outward force but because they seem self-evident to him, and more important than himself. Within such a framework, conflicts can be borne more easily, and I become gentler in the process.

Today our cultural and religious values have become obsolete. We are not only disorientated, but increasingly show stress symptoms. With decreasing bearing strength, conflict situations multiply, and emotions flare. This is why we need to be clear about the distinction between I and the emotional energy or drive. They are not the same although they appear to be so to the naive 'I' who either unwittingly appropriates the emotional energy or is possessed by it, mistaking it for 'my will', wants, fears, etc. The gauge is that the emotional 'must' inherent in the energy is always 'hot', compulsive, and as such blind! Nor is it mine, for we all know we cannot lay it down by an act of will. Rather it has me, and I 'cannot help myself'. Now, if this emotional imperative with its concomitant 'picture-making' faculty is opposed by a meaningful principle to which I can hold just because I value it more than myself, then though there is a conflict situation, I am supported by the principle and enabled to endure the emotional onslaught rather than being carried away by its compulsion, chasing its pictures, or suffering depression.

Actually, this is only a halfway stage facilitating acquaintance with the full brunt of the truly awesome emotional energy. For learning to endure such onslaughts when we would much rather not, we need 'moral support'. Hence the importance of moral strength as a prerequisite for training, and in Buddhism the stress is on Sila, just that moral strength, as the first step. In and during the training this strength is further refined till it can merge with the now also gentled emotional energy; and from this merger a truly gentle and spiritual strength finally accrues. Sila is a practice that remains with us for life. It is a continuous re-collecting, a strengthening process in which conflicts are suffered within, thus strengthening the personality and giving it solidity, reliability and responsibility – essential qualities for cooperation, for the common weal, and for all further development.

Though we have all but forgotten it, this is by no means new. It is productive, first, of an adult or 'grown up' human being. Only from that is further development possible, whether cultural or religious. So in Buddhism it is said that deliverance from the Wheel of Becoming can be found only from the human state. If we seek release from that Wheel, our first stage is to become a grown human being, residing truly in the human state, rather than a hapless bundle whirling through all the states on the Wheel umpteen times a day! But for us 20th century Westerners reaching this full human status, this maturity, entails a second upbringing, or training.

The way towards inner wholeness, the truly religious way, also begins from there. Since the yearning towards it is part of the human condition, attempts at it have never been lacking. Apart from the obvious ones, two European attempts are worth mentioning. Though both failed, this is not the place to seek for the reason for their failure. But each brought forth a hitherto unprecedented flowering of culture, and progressively they are two stages, youth and adult. Also, they arose in times of transition, when a hitherto working world model broke down.

At the end of the Middle Ages arose an ideal, never concretely achieved but rather 'intuited', of some such graded gentling process which eventually led into the religious or spiritual sphere. This was the fashioning of the true Christian knight and his subsequent quest for the Grail. It failed, even before the knight in armour himself became obsolete, but it heralded the Renaissance. Centuries later, at the beginning of our Western enlightenment, stress on a well-regulated, well-informed mind with instilled 'principles' to check the unruly emotions, gave rise to the concept of the 'gentle man' in the best connotation of the word, a man fashioned or made gentle by his own endeavour rather than 'gently born'. It did not survive the ravages of two wars, but the unprecedented development of Western science and culture started with it. Today we are hardly aware that our prevalent mechanical world model has become obsolete, with a consequent breakdown of all our cultural and religious values. Hence the disorientation of our times from which the whole world suffers.

We all long for wholeness – however we may individually picture it and thus deceive ourselves! Yet the actual way towards wholeness is the most difficult venture, for it leads not away to some happy land of everlasting bliss, but right down into our own nature, through the middle of what we want most to avoid and evade. It is also in effect a 'turning round'; turning away from the deception that finally there will be nothing for me to avoid or fear, no obstacle – for though in a way that is true, yet the turning consists in I becoming nothing, nobody – and because of that the whole deceptive house of cards falls down.

In their insistence on thorough training through all its stages, traditional ways provide a – reasonably – safe passage that keeps step with inner growth and prevents a sudden break-in which shatters rather than rounds out the personality. I need to be changed, for to me the face of wholeness is a terrifying one. Only when I truly have become nothing, is that nothing all.

So the way towards wholeness falls naturally into three main stages. The first is in the training yard, learning to bear with oneself, to bear emotional onslaughts, becoming gentler and stronger, acquiring not Bull-strength, but bearing strength. The second stage is maturity, a kind of mastership of the bearing or enduring strength which makes sustained application possible. Both are essential prerequisites for the third or truly religious stage where the approach towards the awesome numinosity of the 'totally other' begins. From far off it seems a shining light, irresistibly attracting. But my picture-making propensity makes it the most deceptive thing possible, hence it is exceedingly dangerous; and so is its intensity.

The approach to this stage needs to be humble, a way down rather than up. In the previous two stages the truly irrational was hardly touched. What is asked at this stage is first of all true humility, the meekness and thus the capability to accept the irrational, that which makes no sense at all and only irks and irritates, and eventually to learn to accept also the unjust without a flicker of 'righteous indignation' or defence. This is training for the third stage only. Because wholeness is by nature non-exclusive, the unbearable and the unjust need to be lived, suffered, for they are also Life. Bearing humbly the arbitrary and unendurable makes approach towards the central Fires safe. 'The passions are the Buddha-nature and the Buddha-nature is the passions.' The passions are the Fires. The awe is very real, and serves as a shield or barrier. This passage is not possible without careful preparation. Hence the seemingly closed door. Hence also the supposed secrecy. 'Do not tell the frog in the well of the vastness of the wide ocean.' No Westerner likes this Zen proverb, though all traditions warn of the consequences of rending the veil with impious (unprepared) hands.

If the second stage could be compared to mastery of the known, growth into the third stage of the unknown needs, as does any growth, softness, meekness rather than the harshness of mastery which is always in danger of becoming rigid and thus sterile. Therefore what is asked at the beginning of this third stage is that the hard-won mastery, on which so much effort had to be spent, is now voluntarily laid down – a humble, unconditional abdication of all that was learnt and acquired, and to set out alone into the unknown and feared, the irrational.

Do we in that perceive a faint echo of that immovable spot on which the Buddha sat down, that spot which can only be reached or found when all the accoutrements have fallen off, where rank of birth and of attainment are as naught? Yet, in order to become as naught, they must have been achieved. In this utter naughting, the individual Gotama became the Buddha, truly human. His invincible strength lies in that; and the light of his humanity, his warmth of heart and human understanding exemplify the transformation of the Fires, their reversion to the Buddha-nature, which is wholeness.

The Parable of the Raft is a very profound one, and applies also to this tripartite development. The raft is necessary to cross the stream, but is to be discarded on the other shore. There are always those who attempt to discard the raft far too early, and others who cannot let it go at all. Both fail, and do so from the same cause; they have not fashioned it in themselves, and another's raft cannot carry across THAT stream. The letting go of the raft is no mean task, is the final sacrifice. It is the letting go of the last crutch one leaned on. Whoever thinks he can give the raft a contemptuous kick has not even reached this shore of the river. Only he who has truly become the raft can reverently lay it down on the other side. He now *is* it.

We are not there. We have only just started. And since life has often been linked to a stream, we find ourselves on its bank with a bundle of dirty washing that we all carry. It has already taken us a good time to accept the bundle of washing, and to find the river. We know little of washing, and care even less about it. To get that bundle clean as quickly as possible is what we want. Impatiently we set about it, slap and beat the clothes, using plenty of detergent, and mountains of foam float down the river. In our haste and inexperience, we soon find that some of the more persistent stains have not come out, and we have to do some garments over again, frustration and exasperation mounting. Then at last comes the big moment, the pile is clean! We bathe ourselves, change into clean clothes – the new life! And as we stoop to gather up the spotless pile, we see beside it our just discarded clothes, all soiled and stained, and start washing again. Whatever we do, we find that our working clothes invariably get dirty, and that after all we are not going to walk the land with clean clothes that remain clean forever. We try to find a way out, throw ourselves about; it is all so different from what we thought. Life just cannot be only this washing. Yet in the end, having tried every escape route to no avail, we give in, bow the head and accept the washing.

With that, we have graduated into the second stage, are now experienced washers. We no longer create those mountains of foam for we have learned the job. Our muscles have got used to it, and frustration and exasperation no longer drain away our energy. So we find time to lift our heads and look round. We see the new arrivals down the line, struggling with their foam and their impatience, and we look kindly at them; they also will learn in time. And sometimes we have leisure to talk with our neighbours to share our experiences. It is a good life after all. We also have learned to take care not to soil our clothes too much, to avoid those stains that are really hard to remove. We get proud of our skill, have become master craftsmen. Now we have quite a bit of time at our disposal. As we look along the endless line of washers, will we criticize them, and vie with our neighbours? Or can we let go and also look upstream where only now, on fine days we behold the still older ones we had not seen before. They are a strange spectacle; there they crouch, half-naked and happy. They no longer need soap or detergent. Their pile of washing is gone; only one or two rags are left and those so threadbare that with the long acquired skill of avoiding bad stains, they pick up only a little dirt, so that a few effortless and almost dancing movements through the clean water at the river's mouth are all that is needed. They chat and laugh and sing.

Has one wasted a life learning how to wash? Has one acquired the skill of an experienced master for nothing? Again, the final sacrifice. Can one accept what one sees, what is so different from all that one was led to expect and has found and forged for oneself? Can one lay down one's craftsman's pride? If so, one realizes at that moment that those strange and laughing creatures, though seemingly they do nothing, very much have their place in the scheme of things; for the words of their song come over clearly and reveal the secret: There is an end to washing when the washing is washed away.

Chapter Thirteen

Sila – Dhyana – Prajna

WE ALL KNOW WHAT we should do, how we should practice, but do we always bring it off? Like getting up on a dark, cold winter morning? One part wants to, the other does not; or 'fired' by something or other, is either pro or con. This 'fire' is not 'mine' and is best thought of as dynamic energy that can overwhelm, but certainly is of a potential that exceeds my normal bearing tolerance. So I feel I cannot bear it, and try to rid myself of this excess charge. I may try to repress it, refuse contact with it; or try to distract or disassociate myself from it if I can, trying to talk or reason myself out of it – usually ineffectively – and if all this is of no avail, it discharges itself in a firework of passion. In such a discharge I am carried away, that is the 'Fires', as this energy is called in Buddhism, have taken over. Even my voice changes in such a state; not I but the Fires speak! This does not apply only to a crude outbreak of temper – the Fires have a much more insidious way of infiltrating and suddenly flaring – as when a discussion suddenly turns into a heated argument, or slowly turns into one by stages. Views and opinions stubbornly clung to and defended are a usual mantle of the Fires, which naturally also give rise to intolerance and fanaticism of every kind. If the Fires take over, they work their own discharge relentlessly. That such discharges are usually destructive if not devastating, we know. Nor are we unfamiliar with the desolate state of 'all passion spent' and the chaos left in their wake, for such a discharge amounts to loss of precious energy. This is what we need to know, because we cannot afford continuous squandering of energy without becoming enfeebled and so less and less able to bear a charge, more and more at the mercy of the Fires. To avoid such calamity, the Fires need to be 'guarded' or contained. Rather than refusing the Fires or trying to dissociate ourselves from them, we need to become acquainted with them without, however, being carried away by them. This means suffering the presence of the Fires, of an emotional onslaught, aware of, but enduring them. For this, we need bearing strength to be able to endure a high charge without being carried away by it. This is how the training starts.

In an emergency, a frail old woman can perform feats of strength that would be beyond a young man 'in cold blood'. Where does this strength come from, and what is it? This is what we are dealing with here. We all know of a 'second wind' and that it cannot be summoned up by 'me', that is, by an act of conscious intention or will, but rather presupposes that I am somewhat out of the way!

Normally we know this strength only in a flare of the passions, but as already stressed, these mislead and blind us; they are the real obstacle, the Fires. But are we aware that the Fires can flare only when the illusion of I is present? This is what the Buddha had insight into when he awakened – hence his teaching of Anatta, No-I.

In Mahayana Buddhism this linkup is further explored and clarified. There is a statement that the passions are the Buddha-nature, and the Buddha-nature is the passions. We must not misinterpret such statements; the sameness applies to the energy as such, not to its manifestation! In the presence of the 'I'-delusion, it flares as the passions; in the absence of it (Anatta), it reverts to what it always has been – the Buddha-nature. Therefore it is said that awareness of the Buddha-nature constitutes Nirvana, the only calm. This means to be re-linked, in accord again with one's True Nature, one's True Face, with the Buddha-nature which enlivens the temporary form which is devoid of I.

It is in this sense that we need to understand clumsy translations such as 'cut off the passions', for I cannot be without them or free of them! They happen to me and I suffer from them, but the cause of them is 'I'. However, if this my suffering from the passions is undergone willingly and in awareness, containing and suffering the presence of the Fires yet without being carried away by them into action or chasing the pictures they paint, then the Fires can and do burn away the very *delusion* from which I suffer, *my* likings and loathings, in short this 'I' which is the fuel for the Fires. Without I there can be no Fires. Thus containing the Fires, suffering their presence without letting them spill over and discharge, is the real meaning of purification. I cannot become 'pure'; only if I have become 'no-thing', is the fuel burnt away and the energy is again transformed to its 'true' state. From the primitive blind passions that flare because of I (not because of the situation), the energy itself first becomes humanized and finally spiritualized.

In Zen Buddhism, this is illustrated by the Bull-herding analogy, where first the traces need to be found, in our actions, reactions, in our words and our thoughts; those traces are then followed until the Bull is at last seen, then caught and with great effort gentled. Great honesty and great courage are needed in that endeavour. And we need to bear in mind that the Bull, the passions, are not my enemy or opponent as they seem to me, but that we both, they and I, are in need of transformation. For only a gentled Bull knows the way 'home', and has also the strength to carry the 'man', that is, the human being rather than me, home. This is not the end of the analogy, or of the training – but it is a long way ahead. So we do well to look at the place where our own feet stand, rather than speculating about what to me will always remain inconceivable.

And how do we start to set this whole process in motion? Right from the beginning we cultivate a new attitude in our ordinary, daily life. We regulate it if necessary, and we put just a little bit of restraint in. The trouble is that we dislike restraint, anything that restrains and hems 'me' in. Hems in what, me or the Bull? But to help us along, the restraint we need to start with is not a hemming in but merely the avoidance of extremes, of excess. That is the linkup with the Fires. And we also, right from the beginning, cultivate a new inner attitude: of giving ourselves, as whole-heartedly as possible, to what we are just doing rather than I doing it, or worse watching myself doing it. In this giving ourselves into what at the moment is being done, we also remain with what we are doing, rather than letting our thoughts roam about, daydreaming, or planning and scheming for profit, gain, fame, ambition. All such are 'I'-orientated, all concentrate on and are preoccupied with I, me, mine, my wants and dislikes, and bind me into a world created by my fancies, estranged from what is! Small wonder I feel separate, lonely, and insecure.

But really given into what we are doing, at one with it, 'I'-preoccupation dwindles, thoughts die down, and then we may become aware of a 'response' – as expressed in a Zen saying, 'I look at the flower – the flower looks at me.' But this can happen only when I am really given into that looking and thus not there! A musician knows this, for self-conscious performance is dead. If he forgets himself in his music, has given himself into it and become one with it (but not 'lost' in it), his performance will be as good as his skill allows, and sometimes exceed it.

This illustrates the all-important difference between wholly *giving myself* to and *being lost* in something. The latter is blind and so akin to being carried away, with the concomitant compulsion. Again, as a concrete analogy, compare the skilled (practised) pianist at one with what he is doing – and an unskilled one who hits the keys any old how in a fine frenzy! However 'elevating' it feels at the moment for the one compelled or driven, blind impulse is being carried away by the Fires; possessed by them, we are no longer human. Besides, as is the nature of the Fires or the passions, if unguarded they get out of hand and result in conflagration with burnt-out devastation in their wake – outside and inside. The 'elevation' experienced in a fiery flare-up is due to the intensity of the energy. True, this is remarkably enlivening for the moment, and is why we both fear the Fires and their consequences, and yet feel life to be shallow and trivial in their absence.

Do we now see why all religions put so much emphasis on 'guarding' a fire, keeping it burning but not letting it get out of hand? And why so many mythologies present the procuring of a *small bit* of the fire as a daring feat, a heroic act? Often it even needs to be stolen from the gods, bringing it back from the realm of the Divine for human use. Yes, a *spark* of the Divine, but it needs to be guarded carefully or it turns demonic. For if in a moment of inattention (not being at one with it) it flares and gets out of hand and carries me away with it – in such moments, lost, we have also lost our humanity. And though at such times we may be inspired to act like gods, long human experience shows that it more likely makes us act as beasts and devils. Escaped fire plays havoc in the human realm.

Thus we are reminded again of the Mahayana saying that the defiling passions are the Buddha-nature and the Buddha-nature is the passions. The same energy but not the same manifestation; as the passions it is destructive because not contained. What fuels the Fires so that they can flare is the presence of the sense of I, of feeling myself separate from you and from all that is, hence full of wants and fears. And containing the Fires in the body which is geared to do so, I suffering their presence, and their burning away me, the sense of I, that is the way to redress the balance. This is why it is essential to become fully human (not 'I'), and why Buddhism stresses that deliverance from the Wheel of Samsara is possible only from the human realm.

So, to give oneself wholly into what is being done is to forget oneself, or to lose self-consciousness, becoming related to and at one with the doing. Its opposite is the compulsive doing, of being lost in myself, unrelated to the doing because carried away. Action from this 'split' state is unrelated and thus never 'right' in response to the given situation. We will find that in actual daily life, the distinction is not easy and needs much practice to get clear about it. There is, however, a sure gauge for finding out whether we were truly at one with the doing or not: the 'response'. 'I look at the flower – the flower looks at me.' Concretely expressed, actions from this state of 'being at one with', are 'right', because related to and responsive to the situation, and so are also experienced as creative, enlivening and rewarding.

Though we may know this, we cannot do it or bring it off by an act of will. Actually, the will itself, being mine, is in the way. Thus Daily Life Practice is like learning to swim. We first try in the shallow water, and only when a bit used to the new attitude of giving ourselves or handing ourselves over, can we conducively start Zazen. Without it, Zazen becomes all too easily once more 'I'-orientated, or a subtle form of escape. It is for this reason that the Daily Life Practice cannot be dispensed with. So Sila is the essential first step, and the constant companion of the Buddha's Way, and since his *Way* is not 'my' way, it demands restraint of 'my' way, of 'as it suits me', etc. By following whole-heartedly the Buddha's Way, one forgets oneself in this whole-hearted following. Sila cannot be 'taught'; it can be learnt only by living it and seeing it being lived – the latter being one of the important functions of the Buddhist Sangha or community.

Being all too human, it is not always easy to follow the Buddha's Way in preference to my way; sometimes it goes very hard indeed, and occasionally is almost heart-breaking. Nor is Daily Life Practice 'merely' a beginner's practice; only a living Buddha can do it perfectly. We learn, if we are honest, from how often we fail, without blaming others or circumstances; enduring again and again the onslaughts of the emotional fires without being carried away by them, practising restraint and endurance. This is the gentling process that makes us truly human.

At that, meditation, too, deepens, clarifying awareness. The impact of a slap is factual and needs no observer; it happens – no 'I' is necessary to watch or comment or get angry. Slap – awareness of the impact arises of itself, and actually *being* (at one with) what is happening becomes a new attitude, the no 'I' attitude which is truly alive in total, encompassing thought, word and action. This means neither 'I'-contrived nor controlled, with thought, words and action at variance. And this new attitude may be remarkably effective in a given situation because it alters the situation as such. The Daoist analogy of the 'Empty Boat' stresses this point – two rowing boats on collision course, and I yell out, do I not? 'You fool, take care of what you are doing!' But if the other boat were empty, would I be thus agitated and angry with it, or just steer clear of it?

For such a turning around, for this new attitude to arise, this change, genuine and irreversible, 'I' must be out of the way, out of my delusory separation which I only imagine anyway and suffer from accordingly. Thus this change purports that this illusion has been dropped and consciousness is again merged, re-linked, at one with the true nature, the Buddha-nature. With that, the Fires, too, have died out for good, for lack of fuel. And so this 'turning over' also constitutes deliverance (not just respite) from all that is I, me, mine, from the loneliness, troubles and fears that beset me. And so as a corollary, because only I can fear, No-I is also no fear – including the fear of death! Moreover such a change of attitude does not take place in some hypothetical beyond, least of all does it place 'me' beyond anything, or beyond my troubles as I would so like to be. Rather, when I have become no-thing again, the change takes place right here and now, in the midst of what is, resulting in warmth and understanding and an outstretched hand. There is plenty to do here and now, and this doing is no longer intentional, not the kind of 'I must do good – please do let me.'

'The Great Way is not difficult, it only avoids picking and choosing', said the Third Patriarch. 'Clear seeing', genuine insight or Prajna-Wisdom has arisen and with that there is deliverance from the I-spectacles of picking and choosing, from the constant preoccupation with the delusion of I, me, mine; in the clarity of this seeing all things are seen as they really are. Acting from this clear seeing is actively partaking in Life, living Life, at the place where one is – rather than standing apart from Life, separating oneself out from it like a spoilsport because I cannot do or have as it suits me, yet hankering after 'my' fulfilment! What is the 'I'-delusion but imagining myself as separate, sticking out, and so getting continuously stubbed and hurt like the proverbial sore thumb?

Partaking is the fulfilment of the heart, for in partaking it fulfils itself. And partaking, not only in the momentary act, but in all momentary acts in all moments, is partaking in the whole miracle of Life, part of it, not apart from it. An old Zen master succinctly expresses the whole wonder of this: 'How wonderful, how miraculous, I carry wood and fetch water.'

Chapter Fourteen

On the Way

TRAINING ANALOGIES highlight what is needful for gentling the Bull, our primitive emotions and their subtler variations. I cannot gentle them, but I can suffer or endure willingly the emotional energy when it arises, practice restraint, the body containing the energy rather than I avoiding it or being carried away by it.

This is learned in the training yard where there are few options. Our daily life just as it is, with job and chores, can and does provide this training yard if we are willing to take it as such, just as it is and comes. How, then, if we are so minded, do we set about it? And what is its purpose?

The late Master Sesso said, 'Religion is to know oneself', and put it somewhat like this: 'If you have a gun that shoots crooked, but you get used to it and make it your very own, you will make the necessary adjustments and shoot true with it. However, if you do not bother to get to know your gun, even if it is a good one, you are sure to miss your target.'

I am the tool I have; I must work with it whether I like it or not, for I have no other. So I need to find out how this my tool works, rather than having ideas of how it ought to work, or wishfully thinking of how I want it to work. How can I get to know myself? If this sounds like preoccupation with myself, here is Master Sesso again: 'Religion is to know oneself – and that is compassion.' Compassion is the other side of fearlessness. And just as this real compassion is not the soppy type I know, so the real fearlessness is not a headlong rushing where angels fear to tread. And mere intellectual insight is insufficient, for it inevitably breaks down in the concrete situation. Hence training is carried out in one's daily life, testing oneself continuously. Whether he makes a sword or a plough, a blacksmith tempers his metal again and again. The Buddha-nature is in all of us; because of delusion we go astray. So training is an inward path, where one finds oneself in all one's nakedness, finds all the strength that carries one, and where one is utterly at home, simple and straight; where the joke that one's delusion has played on one becomes clear, and the light of compassion gets kindled. For like charity, compassion begins at home.

Live our daily life we do anyway, whether we like it or not. If it suits us, nothing more need be said. If not, then why not put it to good use instead of our usual evasive techniques that merely exhaust us to no avail?

So for a period of perhaps three months we decide to take our daily life, just as it is, as our master of discipline. Though we flatter ourselves by thinking we live it as such anyway, do we really? How often do we shunt things around. 'I ought to do this, but not just now – I'll do that now and this later.' What we actually are doing is shuffling things round as it suits me, thus upholding the illusion that I have it my way. Zhuangzi tells us a delightful story of a keeper who informed his monkeys that since rations were short, they would get four nuts in the morning and three nuts in the evening. The monkeys were wild with resentment; the skilful keeper told them he would revoke the decision, they should have three in the morning and four in the evening – with which the monkeys were pleased. We smile, but do we realize that these monkeys live in all of us? We like deluding ourselves that we can have our own way!

Life often puts us into a position where we cannot manipulate things as it suits us, and with that 'loss of power' arises an upsurge of resentment, frustration, irritation – an emotional reaction quite out of proportion to the cause. And it can make us really vicious for thus 'fired' it seems to 'me' that unless I can have my way my very existence is threatened! Tragically, I cannot be aware of this process – for thus 'fired' I am carried away, 'beside myself', and am just not there; and 'back in myself again, cooled down', I try to explain it away. So nothing changes, and any denial constellates the same threat; tensions increase, and things become more and more unbearable. I must get out, away from it all! Yet wherever I go, I take myself along.

So what can we do? In the training, we acknowledge the emotional reactions against being hemmed in, enduring their presence willingly and humbly. Suffering the risen energy without let or hindrance is a real passion. Stripped of their 'picture-veil', the emotions reveal themselves as force or energy.

How do we concretely set about it? This letter is to be answered. 'Oh no – not just now; I am not in the mood for it – I'll do it in the afternoon, do something else instead now.' No the letter is to be done now. If I can bring myself to settle down to it, reaction boils – energy is dynamic, must and does flow. If I now refuse the energy as exceeding my bearing tolerance, and try to get rid of it, it cannot serve me in writing the letter. So subtly and cunningly it pictures diversions, whispering oh so reasonably, 'It would be so much better not to write the letter now, it would be much better to do it later when in a better mood, or not so tired; it is not really so important anyway and can wait; there are much more important things to be done now.' We all know this endless chain. And the art is not to listen to such whisperings and to just get on with the letter. Then the tactics of the Bull change again, 'I am so good.

There I am sitting and getting on with the letter though I really did not feel like it. My training is progressing just fine, I am doing really well.' No, I am not doing well! I am merely deceiving myself, and robbing myself of a precious opportunity, for I am just persuading myself – there being no way out – that I like what I am doing; sour grapes! If honest, I am tensed up – and the body confirms it – for the fact is that I do not want to write this letter now. Nevertheless, I settle down to write it, for no reason at all, not even for my betterment, but just because it is now to be written. The reaction thus unleashed is quite disproportionate to writing the letter. I may have no reason for not writing it, might even at another time enjoy writing it – but not just now when I should do it.

In fact, I react not against writing the letter, but against having to write it now which somehow feels like an infringement of my freedom, my choice, and so it is my will that is thwarted if I make myself write the letter. That is what the battle is about, and I have to be very honest to get clear on that issue.

If I am open and honest, awareness of the emotional reactions is first heralded by their physical component – I tense up. If we pinch ourselves, awareness of it is instantaneous and brings attention rushing to the spot to deal with it. But if my conscious attention is captured elsewhere, and the pinch light, I may remain unaware of it to a certain degree or totally. But, firm pinch – aware! No act of observation is necessary for this – awareness is direct and immediate. The 'bare attention' or 'mindfulness' to which Buddhist texts refer is just this kind of awareness; it presupposes not being tempted away from the place and moment, from the situation as it is, and being open to it. This awareness has nothing to do with forced or conscious

'I'-activity where I observe and comment. The latter is a rigid clenching and narrowing rather than the openness and obedience to the situation. Without such 'I'-bias but aware, there is pinch – ouch – arm – has gone away; the response to the situation is spontaneous and right; no 'I'-deliberation is necessary.

Likewise, instead of ignoring or denying the physical tensing up that occurs in response to an emotional reaction (an emotional pinch!), there is direct awareness of it which at the physical level, at which it still is, can be counteracted or released by unclenching, accompanied by conscious admission, 'Yes, I know I do not want to write the letter now, but I am giving myself to the writing, though something in me (the Bull) is bellowing against it, and there is nothing for it but to bear and suffer this reaction while giving myself to the writing.'

In this, Bull and I fight yet learn to bear the presence of each other without being deflected. Both change bit by bit in such contact, and meanwhile the letter is being written.

In such a 'double action', on a small and manageable scale, we do what we have never done before: both sides are in touch with each other, and though this means conflict to begin with, they are contained within the body and actively function.

To recap, in our normal one-sidedness, I would either not write the letter now but put it off for some concocted reason (but really because it does not suit me now); or if I must write it, I put up a smokescreen to avoid awareness of my not wanting to and yet having to do it. What I find exceedingly difficult and more often than not – if honest – I cannot do at all, is to go directly against my not wanting – and training brings me smack up against this. Veil after veil of deceitful subterfuges need to be worked through until, suffering the reaction in awareness, I come into contact with the bare emotional energy and thus 'energized' can function directly and spontaneously. One could equally and perhaps more correctly say, then the energy, delivered from subterfuges, will of itself function 'right', in response to the situation, and immediately.

So for training purposes, I have to get used to suffering emotional reactions as and when they occur. Correctly, it is not 'I' who has them for they happen to me. Conducively, I can regard myself as their object, to be heated, hammered, tempered by their onslaughts without losing awareness; in that process, both I and the energy undergo a slow but steady change. Bearing with each other, a familiarity and understanding between I and the energy emerges which is invigorating and warming. I become less isolated, more human; the emotional energy becomes less primitive, more human. It is on the basis of this increasing humanity that eventually a merger can take place that is valid and irreversible.

But we are only at the beginning of our practice. So the training starts cautiously with only our little reactions. My normal objection to this is that I do not mind about little ones, I have enough real worries to contend with. Yes, but a good many of them are simply clusters of ignored little ones. So why do I feel peculiarly disinclined to bother with the little ones? Those which I can just about bear? Is it perhaps because something in me knows that I really cannot stand out against even the little ones, and since that threatens my dear image of myself, I do not want to put it to the test? Is that why I so hotly deny it? Of course, I can write that letter if I put my mind to it – yes, surely, but why don't I want to at the time? Or am I again deceiving myself into, 'Yes, of course, I can; small affair, no trouble – but not just now?' So I avoid doing it with good conscience by belittling the *importance*. This deceiving game I can also play by loading all the importance onto *me*, *my* doing, *my* manipulating everything from small to great (*I must*), and soon I am compulsively driven to do, keep doing for the sake of doing, becoming ever more rigid and compulsive in this fake power game.

Why am I so prone to deceiving myself? Why am I so keen to gloss over, not to admit even to myself, that something does not suit me? Especially if it is a trifling thing anyway. Don't I feel that such an admission diminishes me in some way – dents my self-image? And with that arises fear, fear of loss, of diminution, fear of death, of losing control of ... *fear*.

Fear is the other side of I. My (Western) mind, as the possessive pronoun shows, is considered to be mine and thus an aspect of I. The more separate, alienated I am from the springs of life, the ground of being, the greater must be the fear. The more I need to compensate and screen myself from this fear, the stronger it grows, hence the more aggressive and acquisitive I must become. So I am caught in a vicious circle that increases in momentum. The more I evade them the faster I have to run from my pursuing fears which then begin to take on a panicky character. And yet, I myself have brought about those fears by not being willing to admit that something does not suit me, and suffer the consequences.

This is why training must start with small things: I usually have a good amount of resistance against troubling myself about small things and tiny emotional reactions. I deceive myself into ignoring them by belittling them. Now I refrain from such tricks and work with these small stirrings, give my attention to them and learn by trying out whether I can do the small things, just for the sake of doing them, with no other benefit in view. With that, reactions usually become lively enough. This is the safe approach, graduated, nothing extra loaded on, for 'sufficient unto the day is the evil thereof.'

It is extremely difficult to keep the balance between doing the little things when it does not suit me, and yet putting all of myself into the doing. What is required is to learn to do something efficiently while in a state of resistance; willingly to meet and live the emotional reaction against doing it, yet giving one-self to the doing. This is what we avoid, either by not doing it, or by deceiving ourselves that we want to do it after all, for some trumped-up reason or other. For training purposes, the latter is just as one-sided as not doing it outright. The unknown and frightening component is just this meeting of me and the emotional resistance, that is, the energy in its Bull aspect. And the practice consists of not avoiding this meeting but living the inner conflict, which means suffering its presence.

Though this seems to have laboured the point too much, experience shows that it is not really possible to explain it. It needs a step-by-step approach, trying to do it, finding out how it goes, talking it over again. For this a guide is necessary.

Chapter Fifteen

Again and Again

FORTUNATELY, IT TAKES a good deal of practice before we become really aware of the full measure of our propensity to forget again and again, to cleanly forget what already seemed known and familiar. This is a daunting realization, and without the strength accrued from practice we might well despair. But once we have become aware of it and yet continue with the practice undaunted, our itching for 'progress', for 'more', 'new vistas', etc., decreases, and instead we become more concerned with where our feet stand now, and grateful for the continuous reminders, again and again, of how often we slip up, or forget. Now the practice takes a 'new' turn.

Truly, there is nothing 'new'. Even the Buddha said that he had only 'rediscovered' an ancient path. But between hearing or reading about it and actually rediscovering it for oneself, there is a long way of practice. And since there is nothing new, along that way we encounter the same things, the same obstacles, again and again; in the long run, it is not the obstacles that wear out, but the one who considers them so!

So again, it seems as if two mutually exclusive parts inhabit the human body, live in it, but without meeting each other. The one knows, while the other prefers to turn away and act otherwise. They avoid each other, yet also miss each other. This is the longing, the search of every 'I', for it is I, who like the prodigal son, turned away and even forgot 'home'. Thus to become aware of one's housemate is a great step forward. For, neglected, the housemate has turned wild, thus can, and often does, throw me drastically off balance. So I have got into the habit of keeping him firmly away or down and consider myself master. We fear each other, deny each other.

If what I euphemistically call *my* emotional reactions were really mine, I could lay them down as easily as I lay down an empty cup. However, much as I would like to do so, I cannot. The emotions may even succeed in carrying me away, beyond myself. Beyond is out of control; being carried away blindly usually runs a catastrophic course, even if it only ends in a devastating row. And yet, the same idiom, to be taken out or to get out of myself, denotes also a very real longing to be released from too much 'I' and from self-consciousness.

In the training we learn basic honesty and courage to meet our seeming adversary, that is, our emotional reactions. We learn to endure them in awareness, become familiar with them without loss of efficiency. Thus we also get better at executing what needs to be done. How so?

We all know the inner tug-of-war that goes on between 'should' and 'want' which is so exhausting. Getting up on a cold, dark winter morning is a good example. Already late, and tired from this tug-of-war, I finally get up with the two parts still at loggerheads, and no time to get them together into a working partnership. Not surprisingly, everything goes wrong! But if I just jump out of bed, then miraculously, with the body once vertical, there is no more problem – the two parts have worked together. No hurry either, and remaining together, 'collected', the day starts well and the changing situations are responded to smoothly. We can experiment with this. Another good example is time: usually we complain about the lack of time – but if we should suddenly find an 'empty hour', do we enjoy it? Or do we set about 'killing time'?

As we do our practice, honestly aware of how things go, honestly enduring our emotional reactions and what happens, we become familiar with our emotional household and learn to contain the emotional energy. Thus we come across some rather startling facts. One is that if I have no option and this is really borne in on me, hence accepted in the guts, not in the head only, then there is concerted action and I have little if any trouble in bringing myself to do what is now necessary. But if I think I still have some option, I am divided. One moment's hesitation, and to all intents and purposes we have lost, or much time is now wasted getting up sufficient momentum. One could also say that if an 'act of will' does not suffice – and it often does not – the body needs to be taken in. For then we are together, collected, and so capable of correct responses and action.

This is a sobering lesson, and makes us wonder who then is master in the house. Our dear self-image gets another dent and decreases a bit. Such acquaintance is really an asset, for aware of one's weak points one can learn to spring oneself into action with a quick physical movement. This is not blind impulsiveness. It is instigated deliberately before hesitation, that is, before retarding thoughts can arise, hence it is a 'pulling oneself together' for collected action rather than a blind rushing in and doing.

However, this is but a halfway stage; though we have learned a conducive trick, we are as yet not truly together with our emotional reactions. But working with such newly discovered data the practice can widen out and deepen. Very real changes occur along the way, and this is why I cannot see more than one step ahead; I myself change at every step.

From the beginning, the practice is an experiment with oneself, in which new and unexpected data will arise and it is with these that the work continues, which in turn will bring forth still others, and so on. As a practice, it is physical more than mental, for the difficulties are seen to be in the body, and can best be dealt with in and through and with the body – such as jumping out of bed quickly rather than thinking about it – hesitating. We all know that an act of will is usually ineffective if it goes against the 'inclinations', and is thus merely a waste of time, and a waste of what little energy there is available for an act of will!

The difficulty is that however this is explained, however the point is laboured, it is not really possible to 'understand' without the practice having actually started and some of these experiential data having been collected. We live too much in our thoughts of how something should be. This is a very real difficulty in the beginning and entails slogging away at what I do not quite understand or what I think I understand but cannot do when it comes down to it! Or my thoughts lead astray. Hence again the need for a guide. My understanding is deluded anyway, and refers to 'I'-activity; so practice can be quite disconcerting. It is essential to continue undeterred until awareness arises of what the practice is really about. Once started, it seems profoundly negative and nebulous to begin with, 'not this, no, not that', until sooner or later, when all the known avenues and escape routes are cut off, there is a first inkling and from then on things get livelier. A meeting has taken place, the two occupants of the house have glimpsed each other and though as yet wary and distrustful of each other, they at least acknowledge each other's presence, can learn to bear it, and become aware that they need to reckon with as well as consider each other. With that, one is less likely to be deceived by the other, or to deceive oneself.

This is a real discovery, and is like entering an unknown and little suspected realm. Awareness of it arises only after a good deal of effort has been expended. It comes by having done the practice and is the result of doing, like learning to ride a bicycle and after trying and trying, suddenly finding one's balance. 'Now I see why it cannot be explained.'

So the daily life practice continues, giving oneself whole-heartedly to what is being done, enduring any emotional reactions that may arise. By enduring them, their energy is neither refused nor discharged but contained, and becomes available. Discharge wastes it in 'fireworks', and repression affects the body, for energy is dynamic. Thus doing what is to be done, smoothly, whether I like it or not, learning to do so while aware of the emotional charge – this dual process is the real practice or training. It is best done with the Buddhist formula, 'The Fires still burn, I am still here' and is followed with a bow and the invitation to the Fires, 'Please burn me away.' This welcoming, open attitude is a true purification which makes use of the energy to work on me, and so both I and the energy change in the process. Both become gentler, more human; they become compatible, even begin to resemble each other, and finally can merge.

With that, the split into two disparate parts has been healed. Needless to say, this is a very long process of trans-formation, and a guide is essential on the way.

From about the time when the two seeming opponents can tolerate the presence of each other, when I have learned to acknowledge and to bear the emotional reactions at least occasionally, and there is a clear awareness of the physical dif-ference between energy contained in the body, and endured (the burning), or being carried away, then the daily life practice is conducively supported by a meditative exercise.

Today we have a prolific literature on meditation methods, each promising to be simpler, better, more effective. The beginner looks round, reads, goes to this and that place, and becomes bewildered, does not know which to choose. Trying one way, thoughts of what others advise rise up or, deeming his progress too slow, another 'promising' method is tried. There is also the hope nowadays that meditation is the method *par excellence* to relieve me of all my troubles and anxieties or whatever, and that if only I meditate long and hard enough, the miracle will happen and enlightenment, higher consciousness, or whatever I covet, will be mine. But books about meditation, even on methods derived from meditation, abound, and most of them promise 'quick results'. Few such books mention that meditation is a religious practice presupposing a pre-training of Sila (discipline) from which the inner strength is derived to conduct one's life along certain lines.

Thus the religious practice of meditation is neither mental gymnastics nor mental manipulation. The confusion is increased by the term 'mind' with its connotations of I and will and thoughts, thus leaving out the 'other partner', the heart energy that flares in the emotions and is, as we all know, a formidable opponent; that's why we so often either cannot get on with the practice or even forget about it, though we *think* we want to do it!

But then we read about 'methods' of meditation – 'The mind is placed on...', etc. Who places it? Or having succeeded in placing it, can we keep it there? And what is 'my mind' except an aspect of I? So, what outcome can we expect from such internal acrobatics? After the first elation – the 'placebo effect' – is over, the split widens instead of healing. Then, like a drug addict, I escape into more 'meditation'; and become estranged from daily life which seems both hateful and threatening. Again, I need a guide, not a book!

Meditational exercises are religious practices intimately geared to the religious framework of which they are a part. Hence they are not 'techniques' to be chosen at random, even less without their relevant framework. All developed religions have well-developed and well-tried meditational exercises which are geared to lead the religious aspirant to the realization of the ineffable and imperceptible which is wholeness – and for which the religious frameworks are so many cloaks to render a perceptible approximation. Hence to regard meditative exercises as unrelated techniques to pick and choose and change at will is mistaken; the result inevitably is a spiritual hangover. We know that mixing our drinks is not conducive – and neither is overindulgence.

If serious, it means undertaking a religious practice under a reputable guide, and getting on with it without being led astray by one's itch for 'quick results'. So how to choose among the wide variety on offer? The Kalama Sutra, a Southern Buddhist scripture, puts this succinctly. There it is recorded that after the Buddha had preached to the Kalamas, they asked his advice as to whom they now should follow, for other teachers had also come to them, and they were bewildered. The Buddha's reply, the gist of it, was not to believe blindly, but "when you yourselves know 'that these things are good, these things are not blameable; these things are praised by the wise; undertaken and observed, these things lead to benefit and happiness', then enter and abide with them."

It could not be put fairer, and it is as relevant today as it was then. However, the Kalama Sutra does not treat of methods or techniques, but of the religious life; we must not forget that. The flashy, the way out, the easy promise, is not found on any religious way; and to degrade a religious exercise into a mechanical technique surely misses the enlivening spirit. But as it often happens, if I have invested a lot of time and effort in such a 'method', I cannot readily let it go either; then my opinions harden – it must work! Yet, the harder I strive, the worse it gets; the motive is wrong, the attitude is wrong, and since 'even the right means turn adverse for the wrong man', all the more so do the not-right means.

We must be quite clear about that. So which teaching should we follow? The Buddha's advice still holds good. Should we, after looking round and careful consideration find more than one teaching according to the Buddha's advice, then to conducively follow that one to which our heart inclines. That means, to first acquaint ourselves thoroughly with it, then to ponder its formulations in the heart (not in the head), and as soon as possible to give ourselves into its well-established discipline. Only thus do we become ready and capable of undergoing its meditational practice. We must learn to walk before we can run.

Changes occur by living the discipline. In meditation, which then can support the discipline, changes that have taken place become clear; meditation also confirms the teachings which are now no longer abstract ideas but imbued with life and meaning. In the final stages, the practiser 'becomes' the teachings for now lives them. And since the heart of man and the heart of religion, having gone that deep, are one, the mystics of all ages speak the same language – they understand each other well!

Thus to sum up: without being grounded in, and living, a relevant discipline, a 'daily life practice' (and for us lay people our daily life, how we live it, is the practice), attempts at meditation will at best be short-lived and fruitless. If nevertheless persisted in stubbornly they will only embellish I, and harden my existing opinions into fanaticism. Or the wonder-world of the psychological hinterland will break open and even if it does not seize me, it will dazzle and mercilessly deceive the little fool that I am. Which serves me right – hankering to possess myself of the fancies of my mind, instead of diligently working with the daily life practice which is also the refuge from the fancies. Nor is such a daily life practice a 'mere' beginner's practice as we have already seen. Only a living Buddha can do it 'perfectly'.

So, meditative training is conducively undertaken when the daily life discipline is well under way. When to start and how to practice is best left to the teacher to decide; otherwise it will soon revert back to 'as it suits *me*, as *I* think right'. By experience with the daily life practice, the usual hurdles, blocks, and bottlenecks that regularly occur also in meditational exercise may be endured and worked through – again and again, to endure emotional reactions and resistances in full awareness while getting on smoothly with what one is doing. Daily life practice seems simple but is in fact exceedingly difficult to carry out and continue; it causes conflicts, insists on our active engagements and brooks no evasion. If meditation is started too soon, inevitably and quite unbeknown to myself, I place more and more emphasis on meditation and so 'with good conscience' let the daily life practice slide! Then meditation goes wrong, or goes stale. 'When the cart sticks in the mire, do you whip the cart or the ox?'

But embedded in a diligent daily life practice, meditation is a safe and natural component of the religious life and leads to deepening insight.

Chapter Sixteen

Zazen –
Sitting Meditation

WHOEVER HAS TRIED, for just five minutes, comfortably sitting in an armchair, to keep his mind a blank, knows the futility of such mental gymnastics. I cannot do it, and my will counts for little. My very trying produces a counter-reaction. I cannot blank myself out, cannot see myself. 'The eye that sees but cannot see itself; the sword that cuts but cannot cut itself.'

Whatever we know we have learned through the body: walking, speaking, writing, playing the piano, learning languages, or swimming. In meditation, too, this interaction of body and mind is taken account of, and the physical posture is the first step towards collecting the heart. This collecting is akin to but not the same as what is expressed in the familiar idiom 'pull yourself together'.

For the posture, stability and balance are of first importance. Once established the posture should carry itself, needing no further attention, causing no distraction by imbalance and need for correction. For this, a stable base is needed. This is achieved by the two knees and the buttocks forming a tripod on the sitting cushion; an extra little cushion to raise the buttocks helps to bring the knees firmly down. If this position is not possible, a chair will do provided its height is just up to below the knees with thighs well apart and supported by the seat. This position also provides a stable tripod but misses the slightly forward thrust.

On this basic tripod the trunk then balances with a straight back. The slightly arched spine ensures that the skeletal structure carries itself without strain and needs no muscle pull to keep it in position. The head is balanced on top with the chin slightly drawn in to hold it firmly; ears, shoulders and hips are in a straight line, and so are nose and navel.

Hands and forearms are supported in the lap or on the thighs, otherwise the weight of the arms pulls the shoulder muscles and the posture sags with subsequent pain in the shoulders and neck which may even result in unpleasant headaches. The left hand is placed under the right hand; either the hands grip or the thumbs brace each other. Contact needs to be firm to keep muscle tone and with that alertness. Flabby hands are the first sign of flagging attention, with that the posture sags, and vacuity and daydreaming ensues.

The mouth is kept closed, teeth touching, with the tongue on the upper palate. The eyes are just slightly open as portrayed in all Buddha images. The beginner has many questions, especially what to do with the eyes, whether focussed or not, etc. It is best not to be distracted by these but to continue on the excellent advice, 'Better than learning it, get used to it'. Like learning to ride a bicycle, it comes with practice. 'How do I keep the balance?' Explanations are to no avail; I just have to try and try until used to it. Then it is easy; before it was not.

Once posture is thus settled, it remains motionless, and can now be forgotten; carrying itself, it will not intrude. What now needs to be 'turned round' is the wayward heart that disports itself outside, ceaselessly chasing all kinds of things and fancies. Thus we count, the counting acting as a kind of tethering pole restraining the inward hopping around and chattering. But not 'I count'; as familiar from the daily life practice, I give myself wholly, totally, into each count, merging with it, into it. This is 'right concentration', and it needs to be learned. It also needs a pace-setter or the count will speed up and run away. Such a pace-setter is at hand, for breathe we do anyway. Thus each count is hung on an out-breath, and kept for as long as the out-breath happens to last. That is all. If I fail to give myself completely over to the count, in the absence of outside distractions, there will either be the temptation to start twitching and fidgeting, or trains of thoughts and daydreams arise. Putting attention off the count and onto these, even if to repulse them, is delivering oneself over to distraction and thus the opposite of what we are meant to do which is keeping at one with the count. Becoming aware of having been distracted or having lost the count, the correcting device is to hand oneself resolutely back into the count again. And since one usually has forgotten at which count the interruption occurred, without further ado one simply bows oneself into the 'oonnne'. The counting goes from one to ten repeatedly, though in fact it is rare to really reach ten!

Usually the excitement of at last starting 'to meditate' acts as a stimulant, and the counting goes well to begin with. But when it loses its novelty, the reverse sets in; legs hurt, the counting becomes unendurably boring, and up rise resistances. 'What am I doing, making a fool of myself; of course I can count; soul-destroying exercise – not for me! Why can't I have a subject for 'my' meditation, something interesting to keep my mind on; how I could meditate then!'

Here the Daily Life Practice supports; I have become used to the rearing of the Bull when something does not suit me, and learned to keep on nevertheless. Holding steadfast, enduring, giving myself with ever-renewed effort into the count, in weeks or months this obstacle is worked through. But that is only the very first tip of the 'I'-obstacle ground away. Usually this is followed by smoother sitting, giving in to the count somewhat more easily; but in that another difficulty rears up, and so easier stretches are best not indulged in for too long, but rather are used to give oneself into the count with greater effort, more completely and wholeheartedly. In practice, this extra effort seems difficult to exert at this stage, and the more usual symptoms of not exerting it appear; sleepiness, daydreaming, or falling into an empty vacuity which the practiser tends to mistake for his goal but against which all the texts warn. Here, in the language of the Bull-herding pictures, the whip is needed. Actually at this stage the effort needs to be twofold, in the Daily Life Practice as well as in Zazen. By this double effort this also may be worked through. Usually from then on, though occasionally also earlier as a beckoning 'carrot', the meditator jerks up from a depth he has fallen into and which was not sleep. Excitement at it is at first inevitable, and with that it recedes and things revert to normal. Such meditational 'experiences' are best ignored, the more so if they also happen to be picturesque. They occur, but to get sidetracked by them leads back to I and the practice suffers.

Fortunately, since the practice – both Daily Life and sitting – is by now quite exacting, the serious practiser finds little time to indulge in speculating about such a 'fall-off' and soon forgets about it in his everyday routine. Then it occurs again, to again be forgotten. With further acquaintance, familiarity sets in. Emerging from such fall-offs, he no longer gets excited but is content to let it be. There is therefore an ever increasing gap or period between jerking up and I again fully asserting myself, or, expressed correctly, during this ever lengthening 'interval' I am not there to interfere. 'I'-interference, like my excitement about it, drives it away instantly. In the absence of I there is only awareness without a trace of self-consciousness or itch to grasp at it. This awareness is subjectless, thus choiceless, reflective and reflecting – 'I look at the flower, the flower looks at me', simultaneously. And when the flower moves out of the field of vision and something else falls into it, there is again just reflection. This reflection is from the clean bright heart-mirror ('purified') without 'I'-interference and preconceptions, seeing all things as they really are, and totally fresh. This is also the state of real meditation, and by continuing the practice it becomes in time the prevailing attitude not only on the meditation cushion but holding in daily life as well, in all situations and circumstances. And this is just what the 'Zen School' means, literally the 'meditation school'. By the twin principles of Daily Life Practice and Zazen it engenders the meditational attitude in one's daily life in all its activities. It is therefore essential, as Master Hakuin particularly stresses, that this attitude is tested again and again in daily life. If it does not hold there even under the worst or most threatening circumstances, there is still much practice to be done. But for it to hold thus, is it surprising that the 'hard and bitter training' is stressed frequently? To quote Master Hakuin again, 'Be prepared to sweat white beads, to endure the unendurable.' Only by this can the deep strong root of 'I', with its picking and choosing and concomitant afflicting passions, be worked out, and the transformation into the Buddha-nature occur.

But to get back to the beginning, the counting itself, be it clearly said, is a skilful means of approaching the first stage of Buddhist meditation, Satipatthana or 'mindfulness of breathing' as it is often misleadingly translated. It is better understood as being given into or at one with the breathing in the reflecting attitude discussed above. I cannot learn to meditate; meditation is the absence of I.

In this absence, the heart is liberated from the stranglehold of I, as I want it, my opinions, expectations, preconceptions. In this absence, the seeing is the reflection of the clear heart-mirror, and the warmth of the heart can flow freely, which is compassion. This is not the end of the training, but it is what meditation means which is an essential discipline for the training.

With that, the feet are now firmly placed on the Way. The pilgrim has changed considerably from the one who first started out. His heart has become wider, more embracing; he is less concerned with himself because more at one with himself and thus with others. His opinions and convictions are fading away and in their stead warmth and joy begin to flow, reaching and touching others. This is an active warmth, engaged in life, re-linked to the ground of being, in accord with it. In this, the springs of creativity are tapped and the true individual gifts or vocation become clear, can be engaged in, and add a new dimension. The artist will be a better artist, the bus driver a better bus driver; more important, however, both will be better human beings and, joyfully working, happier ones as well.

From now on there is a living, being, and acting out of that. With the dwindling of I and my importance the striving after a goal has also receded, as well as the concern about my progress. The insight arises that this Way has no goal; nor can it be walked for oneself alone for just this very 'I', that would want to do so, falls by the wayside. Awareness arises that every step is its own reward, that the walking is for the love of it, in fellowship with what is met, another pilgrim, a flower by the way, a stone on the road, a bird on a tree. This is the companionship of the one released from I; it is natural and spontaneous, neither willed nor contrived, just there, and naturally good. Hence it is said of this Way that it is walked for the sake of all beings. Its consummation stills the longing of the part for the whole, and is the heart's fulfilment.

With this the misconception that *I should do* good falls down and expires, together with the accompanying guilt for failing in it. For what we truly need is much more than merely *doing* good, it is nothing less than becoming good ourselves, which means *becoming* whole again. From that, action will follow in accordance, and will therefore also be wise and warm-hearted.

So, the wonder and the miracle of becoming whole is that it also means becoming good. Being whole is being good with open eyes, seeing clearly the differentiations and understanding them with open heart, loving. And this is what all our human longing strives towards, however much we may misinterpret this longing through our self-biased picture-making propensity. Our basic delusion is our 'I'-centredness, from which we ourselves suffer and cause others suffering. Out of this the Buddha points the Way. Released from I, 'made good' again and whole, not 'I' but a whole human being with all the human qualities, naturally good, wise and loving, the inborn yearning of the heart has fulfilled itself. In that fulfilment the Way is seen as endless, and in that seeing there is a re-dedication to and re-engagement in the living web of things as they really are, for the love of it, and in joy, service and gratitude.

Hence it is said that even the Buddha, and Bodhidharma too, are still here training with us. We are in good company as long as we continue the training, for the love of it, in the footsteps of the Buddha, and for the sake of all beings and their peace and happiness.

Chapter Seventeen

Practice and Study

IF WE WANT TO BECOME a doctor – or a cook – we need a certain amount of 'experience', of know-how, or of basic familiarity for the actual application of the subject of our 'study'.

The same holds good with regard to Buddhism. More so, for Buddhism is not part of our cultural background, and we need to be very careful to avoid misunderstandings. A useful example might be: 'practice' – I am ready to pull up my socks, roll up my sleeves and to go at it, 'tackle it'. '*I do*'. But Buddhist practice, all religious practice for that matter, demands rather that I *give myself* into the doing. The cultivation of this attitude presents a very real difficulty for the beginner yet it is the essential key for an approach to the Buddha's teaching. This difficulty is further complicated by the misleading translation of a fundamental Buddhist term, rendered as 'mind'. For surely 'my' mind is possessed by me and so has connotations to 'I' and 'I doing' on the one hand, and on the other to thinking, reason, intellect, head. Planning, ordering, manipulating, control are functions of the mind. Sufferings that befall me, and feelings, also emotions and passions that invade me and cloud this 'my' mind, are the province of the heart. In his book *The Seven Story Mountain*, (Sheldon Press, p.205) Thomas Merton found that, 'the intellect is only theoretically independent of desire and appetite in ordinary, actual practice. It is constantly blinded and perverted by the ends and aims of passions and the evidence it presents to us with such a show of impartiality and objectivity is fraught with interest and propaganda. We have become marvellous at self-delusion; all the more so because we have gone to such trouble to convince ourselves of our own absolute infallibility.'

Does this help us to a more intimate understanding of the Third Patriarch's, 'The Great Way is not difficult, it only avoids picking and choosing'? The picker and chooser – who is he? I flatter myself, postulating a 'doer' – but in fact *I am* just this picking and choosing and manipulating urge. Hence the Buddha's insight into the emptiness of 'I' which is fundamental to all of Buddhism, and is one of the Three Signs of Being. The notion of 'I', together with impermanence (the second Sign) which I react against and cannot accept if it does not suit *me* (picking and choosing) constitutes my suffering, the third Sign. These reactions of mine against undesired change or lack of desired change are the compounded effect of 'I' (picking and choosing) and the concomitant Fires or passions that flare up accordingly. We ourselves suffer and make others suffer when thus 'afflicted'.

But 'my nature' ('I') being the picking and choosing, I am thus willy-nilly the agent of the afflicting passions. It follows that I cannot get rid of *them* – or of suffering. The Buddha, on his Awakening, clearly saw into this nexus. He perceived the notion of I as mistaken, a delusion – hence taught the Way out of suffering.

All Buddhist training is based on that insight and geared to that end. Thus Buddhism is not a teaching to be 'learned' but a Way to be trodden, step by step. The 'learning' is by familiarity with the treading of the Path rather than by cramming the 'mind' – already full of notions – with still further notions, the combination of which spawns a still further set *ad infinitum*. All Buddhist schools warn against this. They advocate the Way of practice, and this means a weaning from the deluded notion of 'I', the picker and chooser, and thus from the afflicting passions which accompany this picking and choosing. So it is not 'I' that needs to be changed – a deluded notion is not in need of a change into another one, but needs to be shed. And what changes in accordance with this weaning process is the nature of the Fires; as the notion – or stranglehold – of 'I' decreases, the Fires lose their elementary compulsion and primitivity, become proportionately more human in the good sense of the word, and finally spiritualized; yet their tremendous energy remains always constant. 'The Buddha-nature is the passions, the passions are the Buddha-nature.' Thus the eradication of the afflicting passions is actually the transformation of their inherent energy, strength, or power.

All Buddhist ways of training – and the Zen Way is a Buddhist Way – start with a discipline of restraint and acceptance, Sila, a kind of daily life practice which also entails willing and aware endurance of, or suffering the presence of, emotional reactions that have arisen, without refusing their onslaught yet not being carried away by their compulsion. We can think of that, too, as a Middle Way.

The very decision to start the practice reflects a change of heart. So, from that first step, we cultivate a new attitude of 'giving myself into' whatever at the moment is actually being done. Thus it eventually becomes possible, for example, when sitting in an armchair, to just sit and relax; or when riding in a bus, just to be given into that situation. We do this for a while, and when awareness arises that thought-streams are again swirling about and that we have been carried away by them, away from what is being done or from the situation we are in, we at once and with a firm tug bring ourselves back and once more give ourselves into the here and now – again, and again, and again.

Thus I, 'my mind', gets weaned from picking and choosing, from straying about, and so awareness is fostered of what at this moment actually is. Thus an emotional reaction, if arisen, 'is there' like a pricked finger, and while it lasts, it is being endured without, however, losing efficiency in what is being done at the moment. The latter is what the practiser finds most difficult, and a good deal of practice, of 'experience' or know-how is necessary for it – hence also the patience to continue until it becomes somewhat familiar. It cannot be adequately 'explained'. Nor is it I or 'my mind' that can contain a full onslaught of the Fires; the body can contain and is geared to contain – to live this 'risen energy'. Only I judge it as 'want' and feel blindly impelled to rush after it, or judge it as 'anger' to be got rid of. If our dearest views or opinions are criticized, does the argument become heated? If so, the fiery energy has risen, and the best course is to bow to that energy which factually is there, and address it with, 'Please burn *me* away' – which is what purification means in the religious sense. The energy, being dynamic, but now not refused, can burn away the notion of 'I' which is experienced as suffering, being churned and pounded. This is the transforming process, little by little redressing the propensity of picking and choosing and thus engendering the concomitant 'gentling' of the Fires.

To sum up, in the course of the practice of restraint and acceptance 'I' am not the engineer who manipulates, but rather am given into what is. The latter, however, is the opposite of being 'lost' in it or of blind impetuosity in which awareness is blotted out. Thus 'given into' daily life practice, little by little the notion of 'I', with picking and choosing, loses its grip and to that extent arises in its place an 'inner strength', that is not 'I', not mine, with a neutral awareness that needs no observer nor act of observing. It is rather like stubbing one's toe – awareness of it is instantaneous and arises of itself. Thought is secondary and arises only after the event.

A certain amount of 'inner strength' (not mine) and thus familiarity with the practice – Sila – is necessary to undertake the religious exercise of meditation which further refines and increases this inner strength. It thus leads still further away from the delusion of 'I' with its attachments and aversions and finally into the full clarity of seeing which is undeluded or 'I'-less seeing.

All this goes to show that the Buddhist practice cannot be assessed or 'understood' from the premise of I. I suffer from delusion. The only way to get out of both, delusion and suffering – which is in fact the Buddha's Way – is to undergo the relevant practices. This stands to reason because in and by the practice both I and the Fires change. It thus stands to reason that I, as I am now, cannot see further than one step ahead. Any speculations about 'further on' are merely a set of delusions appertaining to the stage I am now in. These delusions are therefore reflections of that particular state which may be deduced by a set of delusions it reflects. Nature strives towards wholeness and balance, and until it is reached, each state or stage has its complementary set of pictures painted by delusion. Practice clears away the delusion, hence leads to 'clear seeing'.

In the clarity of this seeing which is 'I'-less seeing, the warmth inherent in the human heart is liberated from the compulsion of picking and choosing and can freely flow 'for the benefit of all sentient beings', the texts say – but we have to be very careful with such statements to get them right. The free flow of the warmth inherent in the human heart, just this is its nature – as it is the nature of the sun to shine. In this flowing the heart is fulfilling itself – but whatever comes in contact with this flow is quickened by it. The two are one again – and thus whole. The narrow 'for me' denies the rest of what is, the wider 'for you' denies me, the still wider 'for us all' is still divided as there is a purpose, hence 'I'; real wholeness has no intention but acts from its own nature – flows or shines because that is its nature – and that is the extraordinary impact, the touch that deeply moves and to which every heart responds.

Chapter Eighteen

The Teachings
and Practice

A CIRCLE IS ONE OF THE time-honoured symbols of wholeness. It has no line of progression from one defined point labelled beginning to another labelled end. It is simply round. Pondering a circle is a helpful exercise, for we are very progress-orientated and easily get despondent without visible signs of advance.

In the training, too, we are ever reminded to cultivate the heart of a beginner. An old Chinese master warns against losing this heart of a beginner for as much as an instant (see Section 140 of the 'Inexhaustible Lamp'). And for good reason. A true beginner sets out with a 'pure', that is, empty heart, willing to give himself to whatever is required, willing to learn, to follow the Way, and most importantly, knowing that he knows nothing. Thus he is also full of energy which he calls enthusiasm. As he then settles into the training, becomes somewhat used to it, thinks he grasps what it is all about, he has already formed opinions and to that extent the heart is no longer pure, the energy begins to wane – and instead of 'taking in' ('better than learning it, get used to it'), he is now bent on 'my progress' or worried about the lack of it.

So we need to look into our own heart again and again to check whether it has remained pure and empty. Lack of energy also should prompt us to such a review, or the feeling of unrest or dissatisfaction. The cause for these is within, not in outside circumstances, or in past events which are gone. Such feelings are genuine in that they are factually there. To deny them is foolish. But their cause is usually the consequence of delusion, wanting some figment of imagination, and anger at getting no nearer to it. How can I get nearer or obtain a figment of my own imagination? Who or what is that 'I', that creates such images and deludes itself into taking them as real?

Having taken that to heart, I then try to look into myself – and find nothing! 'The eye that sees but cannot see itself, the sword that cuts but cannot cut itself.' Again I get disheartened, nothing comes out of it, no progress is made, it all becomes just boring. I am tempted to give up, start something new, which seems exciting and interesting!

But if I don't give up and just keep on looking, honestly and courageously, have the determination to do so, then much begins to come out! If I do not let myself be distracted by the outside either, do not turn away, I begin to become aware of lots of things going on inside or churning about inside, somewhat vaguely and nebulously at first but slowly getting clearer as I keep looking. But I may not fancy looking at them too closely and rather seek to avoid it by blotting myself out in sleep if I cannot distract myself otherwise. However, if I manage to just keep looking, I become aware of the ceaseless thought-streams, feelings, judgements, the continuous 'picking and choosing' that goes on, and also a continuous fretting and restlessness that give rise to these thoughts and feelings.

Are all these antics me? Or are they 'mine' in the sense of I having created them? Is the 'I' that thus looks also the thoughts and feelings, etc.? More closely pondered, there seems to be a clear distinction, for surely I can 'see' them, and on the understanding that 'the eye that sees but cannot see itself', what I can see, notice, etc., is not me. So, do I then have thoughts, feelings, etc.? If I have them, if they are 'mine', surely I can then also lay them down if I wish, like setting down a cup of tea. And if I find that I cannot do so, they are then not mine – nor are the problems I may think I have! What then is that 'I' which I am so convinced I *am*?

I am also quite sure that I am alive – but can I see Life? Or 'my life'? I can see living beings, yes – but Life? That is only a concept, is it not? Factually, there are only living beings – they *are* life, as I *am* life rather than 'I'. Only human beings say – and think – 'I', believe in I, and in that set themselves apart from the living context, from Life. What a pity this delusion is, and what suffering it creates all round.

But then, say I, who is it that sees if not I? With that, we enter the Buddha's Path, the first step on which demands at least the beginning of 'Right Seeing' – which is a better translation than the usual 'Right Understanding' or 'Right Views'. But if there is 'Right Seeing', there is also its opposite, 'Deluded Seeing' which is precisely my idea that it is I who sees, and I wish to see 'rightly' which ensnares me in the conundrum of seer and seen, subject and object. But that is already deluded seeing, starting from a wrong premise, from I.

Factually, if you pinch my arm good and proper, I do not need to observe your act nor witness *your doing*. Awareness of the pinch arises quite of itself on impact, breaks in on me even if my attention was otherwise engaged.

With that, a whole new field of inquiry opens – and this is what Buddhist thinking and training is concerned with. This awareness of the sense-impact, of the pinch, is 'given', happens of itself, instantaneously – or we can say, it catches roaming attention and brings it instantly to where it is needed for appropriate, that is 'right' response to the situation: 'Ouch!', and the arm is moved away. Or, if you merely tugged at my arm because you wanted my attention which was wandering,

'Yes, what can I do?' That's all – a new situation has arisen, and we go with it. And if you pinched really hard, with intention to hurt, not only the arm but more, the body is moved out of your vicinity. If that is not possible under the circumstances, there is just pain and again right response, the endurance of pain – if factually that is all that is possible. In all that, no 'I', no observer, no witness is needed. But if I deludedly assume 'my' arm, 'my' pain, 'you' inflicting it on me, or 'you' distracting me from what 'I' want to do, I am caught up in the outside and something quite different takes place: I am shocked, anger arises, I at least want to retaliate (if I can), and am in one way or another reacting blindly, get caught up in emotionality, squandering much energy which only fans the Fires and worsens the situation, and afterwards when it is all over there is still smouldering resentment.

By now I am also likely to be up in arms because on reading this I have got stuck in the 'endurance of pain' and angrily demand to be told whether I then perhaps also should docilely endure being beaten up by a mugger? But that is not the point. All living beings avoid pain if they can. I is important to realize that (Right Seeing) that 'my' reaction to a difficult or painful situation is blind overreaction which complicates and usually worsens the situation to no purpose; moreover, thus blindly goaded into unskilful response, suffering increases all round.

'Right Seeing' is productive of 'Right Response' according to the given circumstances, making use of these circumstances. That this needs 'long and painful training' is obvious. 'Right Seeing' is not easily come by, even less 'Right Thinking', in the sense of 'always letting the right thoughts prevail', thus being capable of 'Right Speech' in all situations; and 'Right

Action' in all circumstances, pleasant and unpleasant, is a rarity indeed. The cultivation of these qualities brings us to approach 'Right Living' which is perhaps a better translation for the more usual 'Right Livelihood', because however blame-lessly I may earn my living, if I then go home and have a row with the wife because dinner is late or not to my liking, that surely is not 'Right Living'.

Thus the Buddha's Path starts with at least the rudiments of 'Right Seeing' – and it should by now be clear that it is not 'I' who has to learn to see 'right', for that is the way of delusion, an 'other way'. Also an 'other way' of delusion is to hold to a factual 'I' who does the seeing, so thinks 'I must watch myself' and busily doing so, gets distracted into thought-streams, causes, reasons – 'he insulted me, he needs to be taught a lesson, he needs to be put right.' The lesson of the Parable of the Arrow is just this – to stick with what is, the poisoned arrow in the flesh, and to pull it out! Which means, for most of us, a change of our usual thinking habits and assumptions, to learn to see more clearly and thus become less deluded. Only practice effects that, continuous practice.

If I stub my toe, the awareness of the impact, and the pain, arises of itself. Who then is aware? Is the awareness 'mine'? Is somebody, a perceiver, necessary? To get truly clear on that is what the Buddha's Way little by little uncovers. Thus, it starts with the doubt about my habitual way of seeing, and by practice and getting familiar with facts, with things as they really are, 'Right Seeing' emerges, and becomes ever clearer, and is also supported by – and can be checked against – the other factors of the Path. For 'Right Thinking', 'Right Speech', 'Right Action', 'Right Living', 'Right Effort', 'Right Awareness' and 'Right Absorption' are the corollary of it, and together they amount to the genuinely clear insight called 'Wisdom' in Buddhism, the other side of which is Compassion.

Look, look, look! Listen! That is awareness, it is always there, is it not? It continuously goes in and out through the senses. Master Rinzai said, 'In that lump of red flesh (in the body) is a true man of no status who ceaselessly goes in and out through the sense-gates. Those who have not yet recognized him, look, look!' But he also warns his disciples continuously, 'Do not be deceived.' For if I think this man of no status is I, the old delusion still holds sway, and there is still much need for training. Why need? Again Master Rinzai: 'Venerable Ones, there is no place of rest in the Three Worlds; it is like a house on fire. This is not a place for you to stay long. The murderous demon of impermanence strikes in a single instant, without choosing between high and low, young and old. Do you wish not to be different from the Buddha and the patriarchs? Then just do not look for anything outside!'

Were it not a common trait in us, we would not have the proverb 'to lose sight of the wood for the trees'. Thus with a growing knowledge of Buddhism, this propensity might incline us either to find out more and more about it (particularly as more translations become available); or, daunted by this formidable array of learning, to give up and side with 'practice only'. And so that we do not lose sight of the wood for the trees – or the trees for the wood! – we need to remind ourselves that practice not checked again and again against the teachings is as unskilful and unproductive as is an array of learning not backed by practice. Teachings and practice are the two aspects of Buddhism. For an overall review, both are divided into three seeming stages, but not in the sense of the progressive rungs of a ladder but for clarification of the main aspects.

THE TEACHINGS

The Three Baskets of the Pali Scriptures present one such tripartition. The Sutra Basket is the Teachings, the Vinaya Basket represents the practice, and the Abhidharma Basket constitutes a detailed classification of the practice so that it does and cannot run into individual interpretations (wild shoots of the Bo-tree!). All Buddhist teachings, even the latest and the most developed ones, can already be seen in potential in the Pali Canon.

For a good many people today, the practice aspect seems to have the greatest appeal, especially with regard to meditation. So another tripartition may be particularly useful.

THE PRACTICE

All schools of Buddhism uphold and base themselves on Sila, Dhyana (Samadhi) and Prajna. Thus the starting point is usually translated as 'morality' – a bad word nowadays when we believe we can do as we like. In a way that is even true (I can jump out of the window) but there are consequences we do well to consider! In order to get the right perspective, we need to be familiar with the Buddhist conception of the Three Signs of Being and the Wheel of Change.

The Three Signs of Being in short:

> Change – Nothing is permanent, everything changes.
> Suffering – Parting from what is liked, having what is
>   not liked, etc.
> No-I – Devoid of anything permanent.

The Wheel of Change:

Seen from the delusion of I, the Wheel is held in the grip of
a fierce demon – Change, and is being kept in motion by the
Three Fires. Itself it is divided by six spokes into six 'abodes'
none of which is permanent. Specifically Buddhist in this
Indian conception is that deliverance from the Wheel is possible only from the human state. Human action (truly human)
is also free because it has freedom of choice. *But* obviously,
actions have consequences, so choice, skilful or not, is important. I can kick a large stone and send it rolling, but also in the
same act hurt my toe! Moreover, this freedom of choice has
moral consequences which are inescapable and return to one,
whether in this or another life. Hence the great importance
of 'skilful' or moral action pertaining to the human state, of
becoming fully or truly human rather than transmigrating
through the Six States day by day, life by life.

Buddhism is concerned with human suffering and deliverance from it. Suffering is whirling on the Wheel of Change
set in motion by the Three Fires, or ceaseless wanting, anger
and delusion – our perennial blindness to see the cause in
ourselves rather than in others, and our equally perennial
inability even if we should have beheld the cause, to work it out

in ourselves rather than preaching it to others! The naive and childish unrestrainedness of the Sixties has brought with it the bitter fruit of lack of self-discipline and the consequent loss of inner or moral strength, the latter being the true meaning of virtue. This is the result of an equally perennial misinterpretation: whenever we have messed things up beyond the generally bearable, an instinctive longing for the 'simple life' arises, which portrays the essence of the human state and presents it as a desirable picture. Hence the 'Noble Savage' of two hundred years ago, or the simple shepherd and shepherdess idyll, all the 'back to nature' movements – in short back to a state of innocence which has been lost, back to paradise as it were – a way which is barred, however, by the angel with the flaming sword. Zen Buddhism expresses this by the three stages of 'trees and water – not trees and water – trees and water', indicating that a forward movement or development is required, not a regression. Becoming truly human involves the fashioning of self-discipline and restraint which jointly produce strength – the inner strength of endurance and sustained application. From these derive the specifically human traits of responsibility and consideration of others, and these lead naturally away from I, the perennial preoccupation with me, mine, my concerns, etc., which the Buddha saw as the obstacles from which we suffer.

Thus, not heeding the dying Buddha's injunction to 'strive on heedfully', we tend to strive on, yes, but heedlessly, causing havoc in our wake, suffering ourselves and making others suffer as well.

It is just not good enough to say, well, times have changed, this and that is commonly done now, so no harm. We use that excuse – for not only do we want to do as we like, we also want to do it with good conscience – or with a good excuse! Thus we disregard the promptings of our conscious which as human beings we have deeply implanted; hence our perennial attempts to bring what I want in line with it. But the bias being always on I, these attempts are not very satisfactory – another cause for suffering of some kind or other. But the fact is that if nothing gives me halt, if I am unbridled, one way or another I affect, even harm, others, fail in consideration of others. Time spent romping with riotous companions, or talking our heads off heedlessly and opinionatedly, we get into the same habits. Truly, the company we keep shapes us, makes us alike, is the mirror image of ourselves as we are. Thus, as the texts say, 'it behoves one to find good friends', friends that truly heedfully walk the Buddha's Way and who help us to cultivate that Way ourselves. Hence the importance of the Sangha, monk or lay – their presence prevents 'overspilling', heedlessness, to which we are so prone. In their company we cannot help but cultivate wholesome habits and slough off heedless and unwholesome ones.

So, with a conscience, we recognize that there is a fundamental moral order, an impersonal moral causation to which we are subject. This is specifically human, hence the possibility of choice in the human state, and with that the possibility of deliverance only in the human realm. In the other states on the Wheel, let us call it the 'fixed' states, there is no element of moral choice; a mouse can predictably only act as a mouse; a hungry ghost as a hungry ghost, etc. Only the human state has moral choice, in it beings can act now as a mouse, now as a hungry ghost, etc., and occasionally also as a human being!

Once more, to become truly human means acting as a human being and that is the way of deliverance, always open. By virtue of self-discipline, restraint and moral choice is cultivated the strength to cleave to it and the true human being is thus forged different from I, the picking and choosing as suits me which is impelled by the Three Fires that drive the Wheel of Change ceaselessly and bind 'me' on that Wheel.

The true human being is no longer subject to the compulsion of the Fires, as with No-I, Anatta, there is no picking and choosing as suits me, mine, etc. Hence it is said that in that state the afflicting passions are 'extirpated' – which is the deliverance from the Wheel; the transformed energy of the Fires reveals itself as the inherent Buddha-nature aware of itself.

But there is still a further consequence: since we are not islands unto ourselves, unskilful actions lead to misery of both myself and others. Or in other words, in the human state we are also moral agents willy-nilly affecting the welfare of others as well as of ourselves. In Buddhism, therefore, these two – ourselves and others – are inextricably one.

Hence the enormous importance Buddhism attaches to Sila Practice, to moral or inner discipline. Yet we in the West attach little if any significance to it, or imitate an exotic oriental form for which we mistake it.

The Buddha's Way starts with Sila, the virtue or strength of inner discipline, becoming human in spirit, rather than 'I'-biased, wayward, self-willed, opinionated, and thus afflicted by the passions (driven by the Fires) and not 'seeing' this – deluded, blinded by the Fires. From his own insight into it, the Buddha compassionately points the Way out of this sorry state – and for this, Sila Practice is essential. It boils down to the restraint of our wilfulness, of our appetites, wants and aversions. Such restraint acquaints us with the presence of these traits inside us, with their tenacious strength. This acquaintance is very different from mere repression, rather it demands patient endurance without giving in – a Middle Way.

Moreover, restraint wrests some, and increasingly more, human or inner strength from the elementary energy of the Fires – by it, the primitive energy of the passions gets tempered, and becomes humanized, that is, freed from the 'I'-bias; not 'mine' but human.

This inner or moral human strength is further increased and refined by the religious discipline of meditation. Hence, meditation practice without Sila practice inevitably miscarries one way or another. The serenity so well portrayed in Far Eastern traditional Buddhist images is a combination of calm and strength. The usual translation for this is 'mindful and self-possessed', but in this rendering it has led to misunderstanding for it suggests that I am mindful, observing like a hawk, judging, repressing ('should not') and concomitant guilt – which are all merely 'I'-activity and not Buddhist training. Hence Sila practice, and further cultivation and refinement of the resulting inner strength, which is not 'mine'. Continued or increased Sila and calming meditation, if persevered in with patient endurance and sustained application, naturally leads to a 'fall-off' of I – the beginning of absorption, Samadhi. Since the other side of I is fear, to let both I and fear 'drop off' is not possible for an undisciplined 'I'. Sila and calming meditation practice weaken I and this is the safety factor in the presence of which the 'fall-off' of I can take place naturally.

Then after the calming exercises of breathing, following the breath or counting it, etc., and habituation in the calm or I-less state – which 'I' cannot 'have', for it just is the *absence of I* – comes awareness practice in its various forms. Awareness 'happens' in the sense that it breaks into consciousness. If you tug at my sleeve, awareness arises – or, if I am wholly concentrated on something else, breaks in at your insistent tugging. Since we habitually are never 'at home' and our minds, that is I, roam about widely, awareness is not our strong point! The importance is that it happens of itself, is not an 'I'-activity. To be 'at home' so that the many daily little, frequent and constant 'happenings' may become conscious, that is what is meant by 'mindfulness'. It is not mental splitting in two, I trying to watch and comment on myself – that rather inhibits true awareness. Since this awareness is not I, not 'I'-centred, or 'mine', but rather a function of the human state, an ability of human consciousness, the development of full human stature is again highlighted and hence the all-important Buddhist teaching of No-I which the Buddha was at pains to implant in all his disciples. Needless to say, this awareness is also a specific human activity, possible only when not carried away by the Fires, not 'fired' and therefore capable of right action in response to a situation. And just these two factors, full awareness and right action, are the meaning of the phrase 'mindful and self-possessed'. Both are specifically human qualities.

When somewhat habituated in this 'I'-less awareness, it is seen as a two-way reflection – 'I see the flower, and the flower sees me'. From this 'I'-less awareness the other meditation practice is cultivated, insight-meditation, Vipasyana. This is specifically Buddhist, and fosters the faculty of taking in and reflecting, in the calm state of 'I'-less awareness, the way all things really are just as they are, a kind of 'I'-less seeing that does not judge and separate but sees things in context and differentiates clearly without singling out one and losing sight of the other. 'Things' doctrinally are the *dharmas*, the 'ten thousand things' both outer and inner. Seeing them as they really are, coming and going, shifting, devoid of any permanent self, thus without attachment or aversion, without any inner commotion, clearly seeing, this is the genuine Insight-Wisdom, Prajna, which is so different from analytical observation, for it preserves the human quality of warm-heartedness, of true compassion with suffering. True understanding of how difficult it is to extricate oneself, further enhances the warmth of the heart which, ever available, can now flow freely at one with the clear seeing. Moreover, it shows the 'Way out' by living it – humbly, as far as it is known, for there is always so much more to learn and training to do. There are no end states – though seemingly 'in the untrodden, the Path comes to an end' (the state of 'no more learning'), yet it is also said that even the Buddha and Bodhidharma are still here training with us. Insight-Wisdom is thus partaking in Life rather than being apart from it as a separate 'I' with its concomitant loneliness; and this is not an intellectual knowing in the head but a living awareness. Thus wisdom and compassion are again like head and tail of a coin, inseparable, seeing all things the way they really are, aware always of the place where one's feet stand, and in service to what is, as 'moral agent' because now fully human.

This is different from just consciously or intentionally 'doing good'; having become good, the agent is less a 'do-gooder' but a catalyst that may incite other human hearts, incite them to turn away from their self-centred, wilful, hurtful 'I'-bias which causes so much suffering to oneself and to others, and make their hearts incline to the Buddha's Way that leads out of suffering into a free and joyful service.

Chapter Nineteen

Insight/Wisdom

PRAJNA, INSIGHT/WISDOM, is what the ascetic Gotama awakened to under the Bo-tree, and it is the light of this insight/wisdom which made him Buddha, the All-Enlightened One.

Dharma is the way all things really are, and Prajna is the insight into this way and the wisdom of being and acting in accordance with it. The Buddha's teachings, coming out of this insight/wisdom, are thus also the Dharma; if these teachings are practised, by actually walking the Buddha's Way, they lead to the same insight/wisdom.

The potentiality for this is inherent in every human being, but is veiled by our delusions – attachments and aversions, sense of 'I' and consequent 'I'-bias, egocentricity. Truly, I am my own obstacle, suffer from myself. Hence the Buddha's teaching of suffering being the first of the hallmarks of all existence, for nothing is permanent, everything that comes to be suffers, declines and ceases to be; and so impermanence is the second hallmark of existence. The third and last hallmark is that there is no-thing exempt from this continuous change, that there can be nothing permanent in any compounded thing, or that all things – including myself – are devoid of a continuous or permanent self-nature, in short (in our case) of any permanent I or self. It follows that the concept of 'I' is a deluded makeshift; failing to see this delusion makes me 'egocentric' – and this is the cause of my habitual over-reactions and of the multitude of my sufferings.

The Buddha's Way leads out of this suffering by means of the twin practices of Sila and Dhyana, which each in their own way soften and finally erase the 'I'-bias, remove as it were the veil of delusion.

Sila, the inner or moral discipline of restraint, fosters the strength of keeping overweening 'I'-appetites and opinions in check. This is what the Precepts are about. I am addicted to having my way, especially so when 'fired' by the afflicting passions with their overwhelming energy content. We know how hard it is to break an addiction, and so Sila practice is very hard indeed. But if practised 'rightly', that is not as a blind imitation of form and not as inner repression, but with awareness and patient endurance, then it does begin to transform the energy that flares wild in the passions, gentles it into that inner or moral strength that can at least ride out, and finally is no longer swayed, by emotional uprushes in any situation.

This is furthered and refined by its twin practice of Dhyana, the religious discipline of meditation. The importance of continuous and right Sila practice for its humanizing effect and as the essential prerequisite, condition and accompaniment of meditation needs to be stressed again and again. 'Meditation' is today advocated as a cure for all ills, as a way to become healthy, wealthy and wise; but with Sila hardly mentioned, if at all, the inevitable result is disappointment.

So, if we feel inclined to walk the Way of the Buddha, we are well advised to look for good friends and guides whose right Sila practice is known. In their company, our Sila practice will be easier to follow, their meditation instructions may be relied on. The Buddha's Way is the human way, concerned with human suffering and the way out of it. As the Buddha's Way, it is mine only in the sense that I am free to tread it if so minded. But it still remains the Buddha's Way, and as that it can, and indeed often does, go against what suits me. It is the Buddha's insight/wisdom that re-discovered this Way, which leads to deliverance from our delusions with their concomitant passions.

Treading the Buddha's Way of practice – Sila and Dhyana – awareness arises that I am myself the instigator of those afflicting passions because of my picking and choosing, my liking and loathing. And the practice of the Buddha's Way also dissolves the cause, the delusion of 'I', my egocentricity and so effects the full transformation of energy or power that flares wild in the passions.

With the sight thus cleared from both, the red haze of the passions and the delusory images of 'my' wanting and refusals, clear seeing into the way all things really are arises of itself, with the accompanying wisdom.

Now we approach the more difficult aspect. First of all, this insight is not mine for it presupposes the absence of all 'I'-delusions; it is an aspect of Prajna. Hence insight/wisdom as a possible translation for Prajna. And wisdom in the sense of Prajna Paramita, as wisdom gone beyond all that I can know, beyond all me, my seeing and understanding, but wisdom itself, as it were, in the light of its function of clear seeing capable of acting, responding freely and rightly – fearlessly – in all situations and circumstances.

Thus Sila, Dhyana and Prajna constitute a tripartite unity, each dependent on the other and interwoven with the other. The insight part of Dhyana forges the link with the insight function of Prajna. Dhyana in itself also has two aspects. One links with Sila and the inner strength which in meditation enables the heart to come to rest, to be calm and at peace because it is content to be at-one with things. And it is in this being at-one that the 'I'-delusion with its constant thought-streams of picking and choosing and planning is removed. Technically this is called Samatha practice leading to and into Samadhi (absorption, at-oneness). This naturally clears the sight, thus seeing from or in this state is no longer 'my' seeing but just seeing – Vipasyana, the second aspect of dhyana.

When looking inward with the heart thus at peace, there is no-thing. The heart mirror is clear and clean. Looking outwards, this clear heart mirror reflects all things the way they really are. This is insight 'before thinking', 'before I', even 'before father and mother were born'. This way of seeing is 'Not-I' (Anatta), is 'the true face', is what we really are. It may arise at first in patches, and become established by continuous right practice. Only when truly and fully established, is action, speech and thought naturally and always in accord with this seeing. And that is the Wisdom Gone Beyond – Prajna Paramita.

The capacity for insight/wisdom as concomitant of the Buddha-nature is inherent in all sentient beings. In itself it is no-thing, no-being, yet it informs all forms. Itself imperceptible, it reveals itself only in form, in all forms. Hence the Heart Sutra, 'Form is emptiness, emptiness is form.' But a human being – and that is the importance of the 'full' human state – is composed of five Skandhas or aggregates, one of which is consciousness, making for conscious awareness. In the absence of an 'I'-bias and of delusion, in this clear seeing of insight/wisdom, *that* which in itself is no-thing, no-being, but informs all forms, attains to consciousness, or, with the faculty of consciousness being evolved and available in the form, becomes conscious of itself!

Only the aware and patient endurance of Sila practice can fashion a whole human being; hence the tremendous importance of the much neglected Sila practice. Dhyana practice with its two aspects links with Sila and forms the bridge to Prajna. Prajna, insight/wisdom, is total – how else could it perceive all things as they really are and function accordingly? It is direct and immediate, precedes all thought, and if forced into verbal expression, needs to have recourse to paradox. Forced? What can force Prajna, the function of the Buddha-nature?

It is stressed, particularly in Northern Buddhism, that it is not possible for such total insight/wisdom to become conscious in a completely whole and holy human being, without the accompanying warmth of heart, or true compassion. The latter, too, in its fullness, demands the absence of the delusion of I.

Thus the whole human being in whom insight/wisdom has become free and clear, does not and cannot stand aloof. How can he feel himself apart from what is? Did the Buddha vanish after his awakening? Genuine insight/wisdom effects the awareness of being at-one with what is, the ten thousand things. However illusory these may be, however fleeting and changing, yet all suffer in their way. The poignant awareness of the 'pity of things' constellates in the awakening heart the full flow of compassion and of itself exacts active engagement for the sake of and in the service of others.

This finds expression in the figure of the Bodhisattva. In his iconographical portrayal, he is neither worn out by his labours nor mournfully resigned to continued existence, and certainly is not aloof to the suffering that is our human lot, but acts, helps, assists, incites, teaches by his very being, fully giving himself to the world we live in. Where else could he go? It is his stature as a full human being, and with the warmth of heart of such a full human being, that is the succour and inspiration for us alienated and deluded 'I's.

So, between the Buddha, the all-wise, all-compassionate, the Tathagata, Thus Come and Thus Gone, and us, the deluded sufferers here and now, stands the ideal of the Bodhisattva, not yet Thus Gone, not yet Tathagata, but here still with us, and by his great being and his great actions ever confirming as well as revealing the truth of the Buddha's insight/wisdom in which suffering has come to an end. And this is seen not as exit, or extinction, but as an ever renewed partaking, willingly and in joyful service, 'selflessly', in the mystery and the wonder of life. That is what 'for the sake of all beings' really means! Small wonder that the first ritual gesture of the newly-fledged Bodhisattva is the raised hand, palm outwards – the gesture of fearlessness, which is also that of the deathless. Never did the Buddha claim that he had found anything new, he merely asserted, truthfully and compassionately, that he had become aware of, had but rediscovered 'an ancient path, leading to an ancient city.' This re-discovery is the function of Prajna, insight/wisdom; becoming one with it is Buddhahood.

Buddhahood is not any 'thing' at all, and so I cannot expect to grasp or understand it. But revering it as a mystery, with folded hands and bowed head, even I may be touched by a ray of it, and so touched and deeply moved, may metaphorically pull up my socks, and find the strength here and now to do one further step along the Buddha's Ancient Path. Step for step, it leads towards that ancient city – for the sake of all beings.